TWO
DECADES
OF CHANGE

TWO
DECADES
OF CHANGE

THE SOUTH SINCE THE SUPREME COURT
DESEGREGATION DECISION

EDITED BY Ernest M. Lander, Jr.
AND Richard J. Calhoun

Published for CLEMSON UNIVERSITY
by the
UNIVERSITY OF SOUTH CAROLINA PRESS

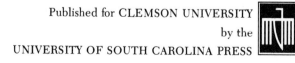

Copyright © UNIVERSITY OF SOUTH CAROLINA *1975*

FIRST EDITION

Published in Columbia, S.C., by the
UNIVERSITY OF SOUTH CAROLINA PRESS, *1975*

Manufactured in the United States of America

Library of Congress Cataloging in Publication Data

Main entry under title:

Two decades of change.

   Includes index.
   1. Southern States—Politics and government—
1951-   Congresses. 2. Southern States—
Race question—Congresses. I. Lander, Ernest
McPherson. II. Calhoun, Richard James. III. Clemson
University.

F216.2.T85	320.9'75'04	75-11975
ISBN 0-87249-327-X		2-9-76

CONTENTS

PREFACE

With the approach of the twentieth anniversary of *Brown v. Board of Education, Topeka,* the College of Liberal Arts at Clemson University conducted an interdisciplinary symposium entitled "Two Decades of Change: The South Since the Supreme Court Desegregation Decision." Held on the Clemson campus, September 28–29, 1973, the symposium brought together a group of prominent humanists from Virginia to Texas for the purpose of interpreting the past two decades and furnishing some insights into the direction toward which the South may be heading. Because of the nature of the *Brown* case chief emphasis was placed on race relations and how these changing relations have affected other aspects of Southern life.

The theme of the symposium was set forth by Robert C. Edwards, President of Clemson University, in his introductory remarks. Afterwards, four major addresses were delivered in the first day's sessions by the following: Ray Marshall, an economist at the University of Texas; Samuel DuBois Cook, a political scientist at Duke University; Ernest Q. Campbell, a sociologist at Vanderbilt University; and Walter Sullivan, a novelist and literary critic also at Vanderbilt. In addition, each speaker was followed by a commentator. They were, respectively, James M. Stepp, Clemson University; Numan V. Bartley, University of Georgia; William C. Capel, Clemson University; and Alfred S. Reid, Furman University. At the banquet session that evening the address was given by Paul Gaston, an historian at the University of Virginia.

Each speaker interpreted the past two decades from the perspective of his own discipline. The commentators did not follow a set pattern. Whereas Alfred Reid critiqued Walter Sullivan's remarks, the other commentators largely supplemented the main speakers' interpretations. Professor Sullivan analyzed Southern literature since 1954 and found it wanting, declaring that the past twenty years has produced no literary figures of the stature of Faulkner, Wolfe, Tate, and Ransom. He then attempted to assess reasons for the decline. Professor Reid believed his judgments were too severe and defended recent Southern literature.

By contrast Professors Cook and Bartley were in general agreement over recent Southern politics. With no claim to originality, Cook contended that "racism is the key to the Southern historical process," and in spite of much progress since the *Brown* case, racism is still a critical factor in the South. White Southerners are not committed to the reform impulse. Bartley compared the "First Reconstruction" of the post Civil War era with the recent "Second Reconstruction," which has brought a re-entry of blacks into the South's political life. But after noting the whites' changing voting patterns, Bartley doubted that politics would "contribute significantly to further progress [of blacks] in the foreseeable future."

While Cook and Bartley exhibited, at best, guarded optimism about the blacks' continued political progress, Professors Marshall and Stepp presented evidence to show that the blacks' economic future is bright. Job opportunities are now open for Negroes in many areas which were closed or nearly so in 1954. Expanding industry, labor scarcity (large outmigration of blacks), increasing black know-how, and black pressure have greatly reduced racial discrimination in employment. In addition, the Civil Rights Act of 1964 had a limited impact. Marshall reviewed black employment patterns in the South over the past twenty years in both rural and urban areas. Stepp concentrated on black employment within South Carolina.

Professor Ernest Q. Campbell noted that federal power, agitation, and pressure brought on the social revolution of the past two decades. Racial stereotypes are fading; styles of deference have changed; the state is no longer "the conscious instrument of those who wish to oppress." At present black leaders are torn between separatism and integration, for blacks have historical reasons for distrusting white leadership. He reviewed the Southern blacks' "minority experience," but noted that Southern whites also know the minority experience—in relation to the nation. He hoped that blacks would recognize that neither Harlem nor Africa is escape and would "settle in to make do here as best they can." This does not mean amalgamation, for just as Jews remain Jews, so will Negroes remain Negroes. However, Campbell suggested that despite the controversy over blacks' competency in education, they would do well to strive "to possess the skills the dominant society rewards."

Professor William Capel expressed the view that perhaps the "other directed" generation which has grown up since 1954 has developed quite a different set of values

from those variously attributed to the South by the Nashville "Fugitives," W. J. Cash, and recently John Shelton
Reed. Capel concluded: "A theory in psychology called
cognitive dissonance has shown us that if we cannot
change a situation we come to accept it and then to love it.
It may well be that much of the old Southern 'mind' was
love of a condition from which it could not escape prior to
1954 and that changes since then will occur for the same
reason."

From an historian's viewpoint Professor Paul Gaston
recalled that the South had long been known as "backward," "savage," or "the Sahara of the Bozart." The white
reaction to the *Brown* decision was one of defiance and
violence. Yet during the past twenty years the South's
image has greatly changed, and the South's virtues today
seem to be those things which are celebrated and are
contrasted with the vices and failures of the nation.

The riots in Northern cities, crime in the streets, pollution of the atmosphere, and involvement in Vietnam have
caused the rest of America to appear less virtuous, less
invincible than formerly. The South perhaps was not so
backward after all. The national heroes of Watergate in-
vestigation are Senators Ervin, Baker, and Talmadge,
Southerners never distinguished as champions of civil
liberty but now known as protectors of liberty, seekers of
truth, and saviors of honesty and integrity. Like other
speakers on the symposium, Professor Gaston noted the
South's need for further progress in its race relations and
economic development. He also suspected that future
historians would place great emphasis on the role of *black*
leadership in breaking the logjam of Southern history and

forcing the nation to view the shame of the past and the racist bedrock of Southern civilization that has been responsible for that shame.

How accurately have these scholars interpreted the past twenty years? Whether or not they gave definitive answers may be open to question by those who read the record of what was said. We are confident, however, that the essays and critiques printed in this volume contain important dialogue about significant changes which have occurred during the past two decades—significant to the South and to the nation.

On the second day the symposium focused on "Changes in South Carolina Since the Supreme Court Desegregation Decision." The speakers were Robert McC. Figg, Jr., Dean Emeritus, School of Law, University of South Carolina; Charles H. Wickenberg, Jr., Associate Editor, *The State* (Columbia); William B. Royster, Superintendent, District Five, Anderson County Schools; Theo Mitchell, attorney at law and President of the South Carolina Council on Human Rights; and Jack E. Tuttle, Associate Professor of Political Science, Clemson University. Because of the restricted nature of the second day's program, the editors have not included these addresses herein.

As coordinators of the symposium and editors of the proceedings, we wish to thank the following Clemson faculty members for chairing sessions: Professors Charles W. Dunn and Robert S. Lambert, and Deans H. Morris Cox and Claud B. Green. Others who rendered valuable service were W. Harry Durham, Director of the Clemson Communications Center, Professor W. F. Steirer, Paula

Bishop, Mac Burdette, Sandra Burkett, Dottie Stirewalt, and Betty Moore.

Finally, the symposium was made possible by a grant from the South Carolina Committee for the Humanities. Publication costs were defrayed in part by a grant from the Clemson Alumni Loyalty Fund.

ERNEST M. LANDER, JR.,
Alumni Professor of History

RICHARD J. CALHOUN,
Alumni Professor of English,
Clemson University

TWO
DECADES
OF CHANGE

Introduction to the
SYMPOSIUM

ROBERT C. EDWARDS

Ladies and gentlemen, on behalf of Clemson University I welcome you to the College of Liberal Arts' Symposium: "Two Decades of Change: The South Since the Supreme Court Desegregation Decision." It will be twenty years next May since the Supreme Court handed down its momentous decision in *Brown v. Board of Education, Topeka, Kansas.* I am reminded that it was a case involving five school districts, including Clarendon County, South Carolina.

I think it is appropriate that a symposium centered on the *Brown* case and two decades of change within the South should be held on the Clemson University campus, for it was here that the court's decree was first applied to a public educational institution in South Carolina. I well remember the day that Mr. Harvey Gantt drove onto this campus. And I happily recall that with proper planning and the cooperation of public officials, the Clemson staff, faculty, and student body, we avoided the unpleasantness that had occurred on several other campuses in similar situations.

The *Brown* decision was the first of several court decrees aimed at invalidating racial discrimination. These

1

were strengthened by several civil rights measures enacted by the Congress. Although these decisions and laws brought significant changes in race relations throughout America, their impact was probably greatest in the South, where racial discrimination had long been legalized by state law. Yet, it appears to me that white Southerners have often adjusted to the new situation with better grace than our Northern counterparts.

Our symposium, however, will not concern itself only with the revolutionary changes in public education and race relations. Our speakers will also address themselves to other pressing issues of the past two decades. As we know, changes of many kinds are taking place throughout the world at an ever-increasing pace. The universe grows smaller; resources become scarcer; population explodes faster; nuclear warfare becomes more dangerous, and so on.

Probably few places on this globe have changed at a more accelerated pace than the South during the past twenty years. Our own university is well-nigh proof of this statement. Twenty years ago Clemson was a military college with about 3,000 white male students—no blacks, no girls. The cadets lived in barracks under military discipline. The 1953 college catalog states: "A cadet must be at all times present or accounted for." Clemson offered no curriculum leading to the Ph.D. degree; the library closed its doors tightly during all vacation periods; no one dreamed of having an intercollegiate athletic contest on Sunday; there were no television sets on campus but there was a surplus of parking spaces; no students jetted off to Europe for special summer programs; there were not even Interstate highways on which they might hitch-hike. Needless to say, the 1954 graduate would hardly recognize Clemson today.

If we broaden our view from the Clemson scene to South Carolina, we may note the same accelerated rate of change. The red hills and cotton about which Clemson's own Ben Robertson so eloquently wrote in 1942 were still largely with us twenty years ago. In the early 1950s South Carolina grew almost 700,000 bales of cotton annually. This was produced with the aid of some 40,000 to 50,000 tenants and innumerable mules. Where are the red hills today? They are covered with pines and pasture, soybeans, orchards, cornfields, and occasionally cotton. But the great white staple has yielded its crown to other farm products. The cotton field sharecroppers have almost disappeared, and mules are now so scarce that they are no longer listed in the agricultural census.

Many of the rural South Carolinians fled to the towns and cities, joining our ever-growing industrial labor force, which has been increased by some 150,000 workers since 1953. This economic revolution accounted for a 300 percent increase in per capita income in South Carolina during the past twenty years.

The recent racial and economic changes have likewise led to a realignment of political forces within the state. At the time of the *Brown* decision South Carolina was dominated largely by small-county, rural, white Democrats. Legislative reapportionment has since minimized the small-county influence; white voters are increasingly turning to the Republican party; and blacks are playing a larger role in political affairs. Many of the racial, political, and economic trends to be seen in South Carolina are taking place throughout the South.

What do these changes portend? What problems do they bring? How will they affect the quality of life in our region? How shall we evaluate these past twenty years? It is for this purpose that we have gathered together scholars from Virginia to Texas, including members of the Clemson faculty. Today and tomorrow they will devote themselves to this task.

Again, I welcome you and wish you a pleasant and fruitful symposium.

I

Southern Politics Since 1954:

A Note on Change and Continuity

SAMUEL DUBOIS COOK

POLITICS is a universal phenomenon. It involves levels and forms of activity and existence, dimensions of meaning and significance, and realms of vitality and aspiration beyond the governing process and power relationships. Political systems and processes, structures and operations, styles and stances are always a part of a wider arrangement of public life, a more inclusive organization of human values, vitalities, aspirations, patterns of cohesion and significance, and a deeper system of meaning.

Politics is a function of culture—the total web or network of what people value, hold dear, cherish, and seek to preserve or change. Political life cannot be separated or isolated from the basic nonpolitical and nongovernmental institutions, relations, and forces, such as economics, education, social and human contacts, demography, family and social structure, religion, morals, literature, and philosophy. The political is not self-generating and self-preserving. It issues from and points to nonpolitical realms and objects of being, meaning, and value.

On a deeper level, politics serves a dual role in life, culture, and history. It is, paradoxically, both creator and creature, producer and product, agent and object. Just as politics influences the whole life of culture, the whole life of culture has a profound bearing on the form, content, and variety of political experience. Politics is an instrument of culture; culture is a tool of politics. Politics is an agent of change and stability, innovation and continuity, universalism and particularism, freedom and oppression, the dignity of man and the misery of man. It reflects the quality and ideals of a people and culture.

Since politics is a function of culture, it cannot be understood and evaluated except in the context of cultural life and values. To perceive and understand Southern political processes, it is necessary to come to grips with the cultural presuppositions and affirmations and the historical process of the South. Southern politics is the handmaiden of Southern history and culture; it was molded, shaped, and determined by the cultural configurations, institutions, forces, commitments, drives, successes, failures, and aspirations of the South's pilgrimage in the flow and flux of the drama of time.

In 1928, a Southern racist historian, Ulrich Bonnell Phillips, published an article in the *American Historical*

Review, "The Central Theme of Southern History." Phillips asserted that the South

is a land with a unity despite its diversity, with a people having common joys and common sorrows, and, above all, as to the white folk a people with a common resolve indomitably maintained—that it shall be and remain a white man's country. The consciousness of a function in these premises, whether expressed with the frenzy of a demagogue or maintained with a patrician's quietude, is the cardinal test of a Southerner and the central theme of Southern history.[1]

He goes on to say that this system of power and social control

arose as soon as the Negroes became numerous enough to create a problem of race control in the interest of orderly government and the maintenance of Caucasian civilization. Slavery was instituted not merely to provide control of labor but also a system of racial adjustment and social order. And when in the course of time slavery was attacked, it was defended not only as a vested interest, but with vigor and vehemence as a guarantee of white supremacy and civilization. Its defenders did not always take pains to say that this was what they chiefly meant, but it may nearly always be read between their lines, and their hearers and readers understood it without overt expression. Otherwise it would be impossible to account for the fervid secessionism of many non-slave-holders and the eager service of thousands in the Confederate army.[2]

Hence I make no vain claim to originality when I assert

[1] "The Central Theme of Southern History," reprinted in *The Course of the South to Secession, An Interpretation,* E. Merton Coulter, ed., American Century Series, Hill and Wang (New York, 1964), p. 152.
[2] Ibid., pp. 152–53.

that perhaps racism is the key to the Southern historical process; it is the most intelligible principle and conceptual scheme for the understanding of the collective experience of the South. And racism is more than a social, political, and economic theory. It is also a philosophy of history, a system of moral belief, a doctrine of man, an article of religious faith, and an ontological affirmation. Racism is a total philosophy of human experience and existence. What I am asserting is the centrality, primacy, and universality of racism in Southern history and culture. The most distinctive attributes of Southern history, life, and culture have been the peculiar institutions of slavery, caste, segregation, racial discrimination, and white supremacy and their consequences. I am not asserting that racial considerations have been the sole determinants or causal agents of Southern history. There have been other influences and factors. Racism, however, has been the basic factor, the substructure, the overriding reality.

Accordingly, the tyranny of racism has presided over the Southern political system and process. The politics of Southern history, at least since the adoption of the Missouri Compromise in 1820 and perhaps indeed since the Constitutional Convention of 1787, and even reaching back to the colonial experience, has been the politics of racism. That has been the essence and source of the tragedy of Southern public life.

Racism has presided over every major dimension of the political life of the region. Apart from the sovereignty of racism in the pre-Civil War years, the Civil War itself, and Reconstruction, consider the Democratic split of

1860, the rise of the one-party system, the Compromise of 1877, the almost endless restrictions on suffrage, minimal voter interest and participation, the birth, career, and death of Populism, th: Dixiecrat movement of 1948, various splinter party and independent electors movements, the Southern bloc in Congress, national political conventions, endless electoral campaigns, and many other routine and episodic aspects of the Southern political odyssey. Racism has been, indeed, the operative principle and faith of the Southern political process. This is, in truth, the meaning of the Solid South. On what else does the historic solidarity of the South rest? On what else has there been Southern agreement? A crowning irony is that just as racism was a critical factor in the development of the one-party South, it is also a critical factor in the emerging two-party South.

In his classic work on Southern politics, V. O. Key asserted

In its grand outlines the politics of the South revolves around the position of the Negro. It is at times interpreted as a politics of cotton, as a politics of free trade, as a politics of agrarian poverty, or as a politics of planter and plutocrat. Although such interpretations have a superficial validity, in the last analysis the major peculiarities of southern politics go back to the Negro. Whatever phase of the southern political process one seeks to understand, sooner or later the trail of inquiry leads to the Negro.[3]

The Southern political tradition, with a few magnificent exceptions, has been incredibly empty, sterile, devoid of

[3] *Southern Politics*, Vintage Books, Alfred A. Knopf (New York, 1949), p. 5.

social imagination and creative vision, and a realistic appreciation of the realm of higher possibilities, alternatives, and the dignity of public life. Southern politics has been the politics of tragedy, tears, shame, escapism, romanticism, sentimentality, memory, sadness, exploitation, self-deception, broken hopes and dreams, falsifications of existence, and self-defeat. It has been full of negativism, nostalgia, reaction, the pursuit of false hopes and vain promises, romantic illusions, cheap myths, war with the inevitable, and desperate and futile attempts to ward off social change and progress and defeat history. Of all the tears of the South, none are sadder than the persistent failure of its leadership in crisis situation, public leadership's abandonment of its responsibility, the default of men of public power.

Brown v. Board of Education, in 1954, was more than a landmark case in constitutional law and the quest for a free society. It triggered the Civil Rights Movement, massive resistance not only to public school desegregation but to all other forms of change in the racial status quo as well. The ultimate significance of the *Brown* decision is that it broke the legal, institutional, and constitutional back of segregation.

In seeking to determine the scope, kind, and degree of change in the political landscape of the South since 1954, the crucial criterion must be modification or nonmodification of the objective status or position of black Southerners. To what extent has the Southern political process moved in the direction of equality of citizenship and humanity for black human beings? What is the state of racial progress?

There are manifestations, signs, and symbols of both change and continuity, growth, and decay. The South is still a divided and tormented self, a bundle of inner contradictions, fears, hopes, and doubts. At the heart of the region's being, there is a power, moral, and ideological struggle between the push of the Old South and the pull of the New South. The evidence of change, at least on the basic and ultimate level, is mixed, ambiguous, ambivalent, complex, and contradictory. There are grounds for optimism and pessimism, faith and doubt, celebration and tears. What is true of Southern culture in general is true of Southern politics in particular.

Progress and hope are to be found in the striking growth of black political participation—registration, voting, officeholding (both elective and appointive), black political sophistication, initiative, and general influence on the public dialogue and agenda of discussion, self-confidence, and realization of the possibility that the political system can be made to work to secure a significant measure of equality for black persons.

Since the Voting Rights Act of 1965, more than a million and a half blacks have been added to the registration books. This means great progress. Yet there are more than two and one-half million blacks of voting age who are unregistered. There continue to exist fears of economic reprisal, inadequate enforcement of the law, purges and requirements to reregister in certain places, such as selected counties in Mississippi, and various other forms of voter discrimination, especially in some rural areas.

There are today some 1,144 black elected officials in the South—a tenfold increase over 1965. Included are 2 black members of Congress, 61 state legislators, 126 county officials, 514 municipal officials, 198 law enforcement officeholders, and 268 school board members. This is progress. This is power.

It is sobering to recall the facts, however. (1) There are 1,144 black public officials out of more than 79,000 state and local officials in the South; this is tokenism. (2) In general, minor offices are held by blacks; there is no black holding a statewide office in the South. There are 2 black members of the U.S. House of Representatives, out of 92 from the South. There is no U.S. Senator, no governor, no lieutenant governor, and the like. (3) Generally speaking, black elected officials are chosen by black constituencies. Whites do not usually vote for black candidates—no matter how qualified. They will, in general, either bloc vote against black candidates or refuse to vote at all.

In various subtle and sophisticated ways, there are attempts to arrest the growth of the political power of black people. Attempts to dilute black political participation are to be found in gerrymandering, various reapportionment schemes, institution of at-large elections and multimember districts, annexations, the malapportionment of wards, consolidation, and metropolitanization.

Change is found in the "new breed" of white political leaders in various parts of the South, but these leaders are much better known for their rhetoric than their reality, their avoidance of the negative than their pursuit of the positive.

There is a handful of blacks appointed to positions in state government as well as to selected boards and commissions. But this does not go beyond tokenism. In the area of employment, black exclusion by state and local governments still is the rule. Shamefully missing are blacks in supervisory, managerial, and other decision-making positions. In particular, blacks in supervisory, managerial, and other decision-making positions over whites is a rare phenomenon. Much is made of the "merit" system by state and local governments, but the conclusion is inescapable that, as in the past, the controlling assumption is that merit is a white prerogative. Racism is often a determinant of the constitution of merit.

In Southern politics, there has been a decline in racism—at least in its most visible and institutional form. This is indicated not only by the "new breed" of politicians, but also by the diminution of Negrophobia, the breakup of the regional consensus on race, the decline of the Southern caucus in Congress, and the development of Southern strategies on grounds other than race.

On the other hand, however, racism is still a critical factor in Southern politics and life. The old race-baiting has been replaced by such code words as "busing," "law and order," "crime in the streets," "neighborhood schools," and "the welfare rolls."

The white flight to suburbia, with all its social, economic, and political implications and consequences, is a grim reminder of the continuity of racism in Southern life.

Perhaps the most dramatic example of the continuity of racism in Southern life is to be found in precollegiate education, which is what the *Brown* case was all about. Massive resistance to public school desegregation in terms of the passage of laws and constitutional amendments—and in some cases the repeal of them—, violence, threats, and open defiance is about over. Three observations, however, must be made.

First, according to a recent conference of civil rights and education organizations, "since the 1954 Supreme Court decision that desegregated southern and border states school systems, some 31,000 black teachers have lost their jobs. In 1970 alone, the black community lost a quarter of a billion dollars in income because of this."[4]

Second, racism is the key factor in the transference of a large number of white pupils to county schools. Third, the mushrooming of segregation academies is a sobering reminder that resistance to school desegregation is not a thing of the past. Consider, for example, Memphis. When a federal court ordered busing, private schools proliferated. According to the *New York Times,* "the number of private schools has grown from 40 in 1972 to more than 85 this fall."[5] In South Carolina, an exhaustive study by John Norton "showed that 111 private schools were started in the state between 1964 and 1972, during the years when public school desegregation was taking place. (Only 15 or 20 private schools and a few Catholic schools were in existence prior to 1964.) Of the 111 new schools, Norton found, 108 have always been completely segregated; they

[4] Vernon Jordan, Jr., "Black Teacher, Goodbye," *The Carolina Times* (Durham), June 30, 1973.

[5] "New Busing Plan Starts Peacefully in Memphis Area," *New York Times,* August 28, 1973, p. 25. An AP account observes: "Private schools that have proliferated under the busing orders anticipate filling their classrooms. There are 213 private schools in the Memphis area, about double the number at this time last year." "No Real Trouble Expected in Massive Memphis Busing," *Durham Morning Herald,* August 27, 1973.

now have a combined enrollment of more than 25,000 white students."[6]

In a recent issue of *South Today,* John Egerton estimates "that at least 1,000 private schools have been opened in the eleven Southern states in the past decade to provide white students with an avenue of escape from public school desegregation. Their combined enrollment probably totals between a quarter of a million and half a million students."[7] He goes on to say of the segregation academy:

Church-supported more often than not, and further aided by a variety of subterfuges involving government officials, it is essentially a white response to racial desegregation of the public schools. In the South as a whole, the seg academies are dwarfed by the public school systems, but in some cities and counties the academies have completely undermined public education and created a new kind of dual school system to replace the dualism that desegregation destroyed.[8]

Egerton's conclusion is of terrible significance to the Southern public order.

The ironic phenomenon of a substantial and apparently permanent private school movement existing in the South while more conventional forms of private education languish elsewhere attests to the determination of many thousands of white Southerners to keep segregation at any cost. With the surreptitious assistance of some public officials and government agencies, and with lax tax enforcement of non-discrimination regulations

---

[6] John Egerton, "Seg Academies, with Much Church Aid, Flourish in South, As Other Private Schools Wane," *South Today,* September, 1973, p. 6.

[7] Ibid.

[8] Ibid., p. 1.

by the Internal Revenue Service, segregated private schools in
the South continue to flourish. The most essential assistance
they receive, however, is from religious bodies that have the
institutional base, the financial resources and the desire to keep
segregated education alive.[9]

Supremely ironic is the fact that the administration of
justice is one of the last bulwarks of racism in Southern
public life—federal, state, and local. There is hardly a
handful of local black judges—even in the most minor
category. There is no black state judge in the whole
South. And there is not a single black federal judge
—district or appellate—in the South. Similarly, there is
no black district attorney in the region. Politics is clearly
central in the determination of the personnel of the administration of justice. Can justice be color-blind when its
administration and public definition and determination
are in the hands of whites only?

In summary, there have been significant progressive
developments in the firmament of Southern politics as
well as in the wider context of Southern life and culture
since 1954. But apart from the tragic continuities, it is
imperative to raise the question of the causes or sources of
the progressive innovations. Sad to say, the significant
progress in the personnel and public policies of the South
have, in substance, come from two sources: (1) the
outside—Congressional legislation, federal court decisions, national executive and administrative action, and
other forms of external pressure and demand, and (2)
black Southerners—with a handful of scattered Southern
white allies who understood the essentials of enlightened

---

[9] Ibid., p. 7.

self-interest, if not always the requirements of justice. Virtually no initiative, positive action, or constructive commitment has come from the white South, especially its public leadership. At best, what has come from the white South has been technical adjustment and formal accommodation rather than substantive involvement.

The evidence suggests that white Southerners still are not committed to the reform impulse and norm, internal initiative, self-legislation for a more inclusive human community, a positive plan, and a creative method of dealing with racial injustice and oppression.

Essential is a movement for social reform and change on the part of white Southerners, with the objective of using race consciousness creatively as it was used destructively for three and a half centuries. This entails conscious, deliberate, and sustained effort. It requires, first of all, honest self-confrontation and self-criticism. Racism and its tragic legacy must be met head-on, creatively, imaginatively, honestly, comprehensively, and sustainedly. It is time for the South to face "the issue" that has consumed it for so long and prevented it from dealing with the real issues such as poverty, topflight educational quality, and the "Good Life." In some quarters there is talk of a "postracial" South. Such talk is misguided and radically premature. Let us first get rid of the racist South.

The South is in desperate need of healing and the reconciliation of man and man, black humanity and white humanity. Justice is a necessary condition thereof. Indispensable are a creedal revolution, a revolution of fundamental belief about humanity, about persons, about all human beings as equal centers and bearers of meaning and value, a revolutionary discovery of the ultimate meaning and dimensions of genuine, all-inclusive human community. "There is some region in every man," said Howard Thurman, "that listens for the sound of the genuine in other men."[10] "If men cannot refer to a common value, recognized by all as existing in each one," asserted Camus, "then man is incomprehensible to man."[11]

Southern politics is in need of cleansing and liberation from bondage of the past. A spirit, philosophy, program, and public policy of humanitarian reform and social reconstruction are an urgent moral imperative. We, in the South, need desperately to move toward a truly, creative, humanistic, pluralistic, open, and free society, political system, and humane community built on the institutionalized recognition of equality of personhood and citizenship. Authentic humanism is the key—a society of free, whole, responsible, and equal human beings belonging to each other, in genuine community, as human beings, whole persons. It is time for the South to be committed to the right agenda, the proper priorities, the creative vision of the victory of its best self over its worst self.

The resources for the creation and maintenance of the "Good Life" in the "Good Society" are within the existential experience of white Southerners and black Southerners—the sense of community and place, the sense of history, the inheritance of poverty, defeat, despair, alienation, inwardness, loneliness, the framework of human frailty and folly, and the sense of tragedy.

[10] Howard Thurman, *The Luminous Darkness,* Harper & Row (New York, 1965), p. 38.
[11] Albert Camus, *The Rebel,* Vintage Books (New York, 1954), p. 23.

Can the South redeem the past? Can Southern politics be a vital instrument of Southern liberation and redemption? A sense of moral and social urgency is indispensable to the transformation of the South. But it is in the nature of things and the logic of politics that such a sense of urgency must come from outside the political order. The necessary humanistic impulse and imperative must issue from the broad reaches of Southern life and culture, the South's truly moral and aspiring self.

Comments by NUMAN V. BARTLEY

The 60s was a period of sweeping change, in the nation, and especially in the South. Black Southerners accomplished broad and important gains, in civil rights and the prerogatives of citizenship and in political participation, both in voting and officeholding. Negroes were still poor, relative to whites, but the avenues of economic advancement were more open than they ever had been before. The South made notable strides in the field of education, especially in the education of black youngsters. White Southerners, in the main, opposed many of these changes—sometimes with violence—but by the early 70s, federal pressures, among other things, had seemingly led most white Southerners to accept, if at times grudgingly, a new status for blacks in society. At the same time the changing definition of minority rights spread outside the South and exposed the extent of white racism, and no small degree of hypocrisy, on the part of non-Southern whites. This convergence of opinion suggested the decline of the sharp sectional conflict that had marked the strife-torn 50s and early 60s.

Nationally, the 60s was a period of immense political change; indeed, the decade saw the formation of a new party system, which included the spread of the Republican party southward, often resulting in sharp electoral conflict on the state and local level. By the early 70s, politics was also marked by highly publicized political scandal, with aides and advisors close to the President being implicated and the Vice President of the United States in danger of being confronted with impeachment proceedings in Congress for allegedly accepting bribes in exchange for favors to a construction firm.

This period was of course the period of the First Reconstruction—the 1860s and the early 1870s. Being an historian, I cannot resist drawing analogies from the past, and there is, in fact, a great deal of similarity, as well as some important differences, between where we are now and where we were about one hundred years ago. Without making too much of this comparison, there does seem to be one point that is to me quite disturbing, and one that I would like briefly to examine within the context of Professor Cook's discussion. Finding little in Professor Cook's paper with which to disagree, these comments are more in the form of a footnote than a critique to his broader analysis.

The First Reconstruction ended with Southern voters rather sharply polarized along racial lines. When the Bourbon Democrats "redeemed" the South by "restoring home rule," they did so on a political base composed almost entirely of white voters. Black Southerners, for the most part, remained loyal to the party of Lincoln and Emancipation. While there were black Democrats and even more white Republicans, the basic lines were racial, with the white man's party—the Democrats—dominating the region's politics, thus largely isolating blacks in the outmanned Republican party.

Today, in the aftermath of the Second Reconstruction,

similar trends are apparent. Once again fundamental
changes in the patterns of race relations have crucially
influenced voter behavior. To be sure, political polariza-
tion along racial lines is substantially less now than
a century ago, and, ironically, the political parties
—Democrats and Republicans—have in this context
traded places. But the trends in political behavior seem
to be clear.

The majority of white Southerners no longer consider
themselves to be Democrats. Opinion research, in this
case Survey Research Center data, reveals that whereas
in 1952 almost three-quarters of white Southerners iden-
tified themselves as Democrats, by 1960 this percentage
had declined to approximately 61 percent, and by 1970
was down to 44 percent. This rather dramatic shift in party
identification was true for both upper and lower income
groups in the white population, though working class
whites were still slightly more likely (by a few percentage
points) to call themselves Democrats than were upper
income whites. Blacks, on the other hand, have become
more Democratic. In 1960 approximately 55 percent of
black Southerners called themselves Democrats; by 1970
this figure had increased to about 80 percent. As blacks
shifted into the Democratic party, whites left it. These
white Southerners did not, for the most part, move into
the Republican party. They became Independents.
About 38 percent of Southern whites identify themselves
as Independents.

This attitudinal gap between whites and blacks, not
only on the question of party identification, but also on a
range of fundamental social and economic issues, has

widened consistently during the past two decades, with blacks becoming more liberal and change-oriented and whites more conservative and anti-change in outlook. The most dramatic attitudinal divergence has occurred between blacks and lower income whites, who in the 1950s shared favorable views toward New Deal-type socioeconomic reform. But while black support for social welfare measures has increased, lower income white endorsement of economic liberalism has declined sharply. To be sure, opinion polls also reflect the fact that Southern whites no longer endorse segregation, generally speaking, and have come to accept many of the social changes initiated during the 1950s and 1960s. But if the question is rephrased into an inquiry about future civil rights progress, the gap between whites and blacks reappears.

The divergence of opinion between Southern whites and blacks is also reflected in voting behavior. During the 1950s and into the early 1960s, the normal voter division in partisan elections found affluent urban-suburban whites casting ballots for the GOP, while rural and working-class whites and, usually, blacks supported the Democrats. But this New Deal coalition of blacks and rural and lower-income whites has obviously collapsed in presidential politics. The coalition disintegrated in 1964 in the five states of the Deep South (though not in the states of the peripheral South). Republican Barry Goldwater won about three-quarters of the votes cast in predominantly white precincts in Columbia, South Carolina, and well over 80 percent of those in Charleston, for example, while Democrat Lyndon Johnson was virtually the unanimous choice in the black precincts in both cities. In 1968 Democrat Hubert H. Humphrey won only 31 percent of the votes cast in the eleven Southern states, to trail both Richard Nixon and George Wallace. Humphrey ran well only among black voters, as well as among such numerically limited minorities as Chicanos (located mainly in Texas), Jewish voters (concentrated in Florida), and liberal whites (who are extremely hard to find). In both Columbia and Charleston, Humphrey carried better than 95 percent of the ballots cast in black precincts; he failed to win as many as one of every five votes in white neighborhoods. Nixon and Wallace split the bulk of votes cast by whites, with Nixon faring best in affluent urban-suburban communities and Wallace appealing well to lower-income whites, especially those residing in rural areas. The Democrats reached a new nadir in 1972 when George McGovern won less than 30 percent of the Southern vote. Like Humphrey, his basic support came from the black community. In Columbia, McGovern won approximately 95 percent in black districts and about 20 percent in white precincts. In Charleston he lost less than 15 percent of the votes from black precincts and won less than 15 percent of the ballots from white boxes.

The Democratic party has fared considerably better in Southern state politics than it has on the presidential level. Nevertheless the overall trends in voter behavior are similar. If I may again use South Carolina as an example, the first serious Republican challenge for a major state-level office in recent years was the campaign of journalist William D. Workman for a United States Senate seat in 1962. Workman fared extremely well in upper and upper-middle income white neighborhoods in the cities, he did not do so well in lower and lower-middle income white precincts nor in rural areas, especially those rural counties of the predominantly white Piedmont area, and he lost heavily in urban black precincts to trail the late Democratic Senator Olin D. Johnston by a substantial margin. But in more recent partisan campaigns, these class-based voting alignments have disintegrated, as serious Republican contenders have rather consistently won a majority of the votes cast by white South Carolinians, although only the inimitable J. Strom Thurmond has been able to do so by sufficiently substantial margins to overcome virtually united black opposition.

And these same tendencies are broadly characteristic of the South generally. There are of course numerous exceptions, as one would expect in such a fluid political environment. The success of States Rights Democrats, such as Lester Maddox in my own state of Georgia, and such New South Democrats as Ruben Askew in Florida, demonstrates both the diversity and the staying power of Southern Democrats, while in the upper South moderate Republicans have sometimes attracted substantial, if rarely majority, support from black voters. But the overall pattern of a politics with racial divisions a central feature is clear.

In pointing out this trend, I do not necessarily mean to project it into the future. Predictions about Southern politics have a way of going awry. But political behavior during the past two decades would certainly suggest that some of the same political dynamics that prevailed a century ago are evident today. Of course, there is nothing inherently wrong with blacks belonging to one party and whites to another. Indeed it could be argued and has been, sometimes from an explicit black power perspective, that such a politics would best serve black interests. I personally find this a rather dubious proposition. In retrospect, that system did not work very well in the late nineteenth century in terms of the ability of black voters to translate political participation into the achievement of broader objectives in society. Given all of this, these comments must necessarily end on a pessimistic note, as did Professor Cook's paper. I personally do not anticipate that the reentry of blacks into the political process is going to lead to substantial policy gains for black Southerners. Certainly we have come a long way from the days of disfranchisement and Jim Crow; but I am not at all sure that politics is going to contribute significantly to further progress in the foreseeable future.

II

Black Employment in the South

Since 1954

RAY MARSHALL

M Y ASSIGNMENT, to discuss black employment changes in the South since 1954, is a difficult one for a variety of reasons. For one thing, I have been asked to pay particular attention to the effects of the 1954 Supreme Court desegregation decision and other laws and legal actions. It is always difficult to measure the effect of any particular force—like a court decision—on something as complex as racial employment patterns. We simply do not have analytical tools powerful enough to measure these kinds of causes and effects with much precision, because it is difficult to make unbiased measurements while holding all other things constant. Nevertheless, we have some useful analytical tools which permit us to present pretty strong evidence on causes and effects.

My assignment also is complicated by the fact that discussions of racial questions evoke strong emotional responses which make it difficult to communicate clearly. There is a danger in analyzing such changes that some groups will argue from the same evidence that there has been no basic change while others argue, equally erroneously, in my opinion, that discrimination collapsed during the 1960s.

People who take these strong views are in some sense political allies—the "no change" group encourages inaction, because if we really have not made much progress, those attempting to bring it about would become frustrated and either withdraw or ally themselves with those who advocate "revolutionary changes." On the other hand, those who argue that discrimination has collapsed tend to induce inaction by creating the mistaken impression that the problem has been solved.

It seems to me that neither of these positions is accurate—black income and employment positions have improved, particularly since the mid-1960s, but blacks have a long way to go to achieve equality of employment patterns with whites, because blacks remain much more heavily concentrated in low-status and low-wage jobs.

It is not easy to account for the employment changes during the 1960s, but I think it would be wrong to conclude that discrimination collapsed because of the enforcement of the Civil Rights Act of 1964. This is a tempting conclusion, because of the timing of the law and the relative changes that took place, but the same forces probably produced both the law and the employment changes. The Civil Rights Act was important, of course, but enforcement efforts have not been too significant.

Probably the basic influence of the law is to serve as an attitudinal barometer which presumably represents the sentiments of a majority of the people, giving the law a certain moral power causing people concerned about moral things to bring their actions into conformity with it, whether or not they have been prosecuted under the law. The temptation for "voluntary" compliance is particularly strong when social practices have prevented people from acting in their economic interests. It might be argued, for example, that government pressures brought about the integration of employment in the South's textile industry during the 1960s, but the truth is that tight labor markets and the movement of whites out of textiles into higher paying industries gave employers powerful motives to hire blacks. The law therefore gave these employers an "excuse" to do what their economic interests inclined them to do anyway. The law thus "protects" employers from white workers who might object to racial integration. (In assessing the impact of law, we also should note that forces to erode discrimination had been under way in the textile industry long before the Civil Rights Act was passed.)

This paper will attempt to outline the basic racial employment patterns as they existed in the South around 1950 and will then discuss some of the forces bringing about changes. Because of time limitations, I am forced to generalize and thus obscure differences within the region and in directions counter to the generalized trends.

The Patterns around 1950

Employment patterns in the South around 1950 were deeply rooted in the traditional South. The characteristics of this traditional South were most fully developed around 1900, after the Civil War and Reconstruction had produced considerable social ferment. The traditional South could be defined by a number of general characteristics, including institutionalized segregation, a one-party political system where race was a dominant political issue, a negative federalism which caused Southern political leaders to oppose national programs that were in the best interest of many of the region's people, low percentages of foreign-born and non-Protestants in its population, low incomes, high percentages of black to total population, and an economy based largely on agriculture, with the plantation and sharecropping prominent features of the system.

The agrarian-dominated system gave little attention to human resource development. Indeed, it can be argued that agricultural employers often were motivated to provide agricultural workers and sharecroppers with very limited educations in order to keep taxes down and to limit the mobility of labor (which limited education or training would do) in order to maintain a supply of agricultural workers to meet peak demands. Of course, the workers bore the cost of this system in the form of low wages, unemployment, and underemployment. Keeping large enough supplies of labor around to meet peak demands, usually at harvest time, caused low annual productivity and incomes for agricultural workers.

Moreover, the sharecropping system provided little incentive for sharecroppers to improve either themselves or the land, since improvements went to the landowners.

Outside agriculture, blacks fared little better. They were confined pretty much to menial, low-wage jobs. Blacks were pretty much excluded from skilled craft jobs in construction, printing, railroads, and other industries. Black craftsmen and professionals were confined largely to work in black neighborhoods or lower status sectors like home building and repair work. In manufacturing, blacks were confined mainly to labor pools or custodial jobs regardless of education or qualifications, whereas whites were hired into lines of progression with upward mobility.

An understanding of the changes in employment patterns since 1954 requires some conception of the main forces causing those patterns in the first place. A basic cause of black employment patterns was discrimination, both overt and institutionalized. The main motive for employment discrimination by employers and white workers was status, plus some economic motive—profits for employers and job control for white workers. Blacks were considered to be "inferior" people who would threaten the status of whites in the skilled trades. Whites tended to use their power to monopolize the status jobs for themselves. The extent to which whites succeeded in restricting blacks to traditional jobs depended largely on the supplies of black labor to meet the labor demands of employers who hired blacks in nontraditional jobs. In cases like cement masons and bricklayers, blacks were too numerous to be excluded, because many slaves were

trained in these occupations. There were and are many
black workers in these trades because whites could not
exclude them from jobs and on-the-job training opportunities. In newer trades or those with changing tech-
nologies requiring some academic training, such as elec-
trical work, no slaves were trained and whites could
monopolize the trades by controlling training.

Employers, who are motivated mainly by profits, ordinarily had few status reasons for excluding blacks, but
they refused to hire them in nontraditional jobs because
they feared the reaction of white customers or workers.
White workers could be neutralized by large enough
supplies of qualified blacks to replace those who quit or
struck to protest the hiring of blacks in nontraditional
jobs. Whether or not whites quit in such cases ordinarily
depended on how good the jobs were—whites rarely quit
good jobs for racial reasons. Employers had few status
motives for not hiring blacks in blue-collar jobs, but they
systematically excluded blacks from white-collar jobs
leading to managerial occupations where management's
status would be threatened.

Discrimination became institutionalized in the South
around 1900, causing strong societal pressures to make it
very difficult for the patterns to be changed. Because
of institutional segregation, blacks attended inferior
schools, lived in segregated neighborhoods, and rarely
learned about the better job opportunities controlled by
whites. Institutional discrimination caused blacks to avoid
applying for jobs where they would be refused employment; institutional discrimination therefore made
specific, overt discrimination unnecessary. I do not wish
to give the impression, however, that institutional dis-

crimination can be neatly separated in practice from overt discrimination, because employers familiar with the institutionalized forms could practice overt discrimination by refusing, for example, to recruit in places where blacks were likely to be found.

Institutionalized discrimination also made it possible for employers to practice *statistical discrimination*, because they assigned lower probabilities to selecting qualified blacks than to selecting qualified whites on the basis of education or other so-called "objective" labor market characteristics. In other words, statistical discrimination accomplished the same result as overt discrimination based on objective "measurable" qualifications which gave higher marks to whites than to blacks.

These were the basic employment patterns in the South at the time of the Supreme Court desegregation decision in 1954. However, the patterns were never rigid, and considerable change had taken place between 1900 and 1954. Probably the two most important forces for change were (1) industrialization of the South, including the mechanization of agriculture, the growth of manufacturing, and the development of communications and transportation facilities; and (2) the migration of blacks out of agriculture and the rural South into urban areas, North and South.

Industrialization had eroded traditional agricultural values in the South because of its requirements for higher education and skills more broadly distributed throughout the society. Industrial societies also tend to be more open than agricultural societies, because there is a tendency for industrial workers to be assigned to jobs because of merit and not because of race, class, or status. Industrial societies also tend to be pluralistic, since industrialization causes the emergence of such group interests as industrial workers, professionals, and businessmen. It is therefore very difficult to maintain a one-party political system in an industrial society. Consequently the South had produced a labor movement and some Republicans by 1954.

Migration of blacks out of the South, which accelerated around World War I because of the labor shortages created by the war and the cessation of European immigration, set in motion a number of forces for change. First, black political power increased as blacks moved out of areas where they were denied the right to vote into areas where they not only could vote but often were the balance of power between the Democratic and Republican parties. Because they could not make it in urban employment with a sharecropper's education and because public policies were becoming so important to their welfare, blacks demanded education and the right to vote.

Second, migration also demonstrated the nature of race relations in other areas. In the North, whites preached racial equality but often fled to the suburbs when blacks moved into their neighborhoods. No matter how bad conditions were in the South, blacks could hold onto the dream that they could escape to the North. But by 1954, it was clear that discrimination was a problem in the North as well as in the South. Indeed, in many ways, conditions were worse for blacks in the North than in the South.

In the South, blacks had institutions they controlled and held the better jobs in black neighborhoods, both of which are less likely to be the case in the North, where many of the good jobs in the ghetto are controlled by whites. Outside the South, Southern migrants had relatively high incomes at first; indeed, black migrants make out better in terms of income and employment than blacks with the same characteristics who were born in the North or who moved there from other Northern areas. However, blacks who have been in Northern areas for a generation do not do as well, apparently because some of them acquire different values about the menial, low-wage jobs available to them there. The North probably looks worse to blacks now than it did in 1954, and the South probably looks better. Opinion surveys suggest that blacks perceive more progress in the metropolitan South since that time than they do in the metropolitan North.

Employment Changes

My information on black employment changes since 1950 comes from a study recently completed for the U.S. Department of Labor and the Equal Employment Opportunity Commission. (This study, *Black Employment in the South*, was published in 1974 by Olympus Publishing Company.) Because it covered so many different subjects, it would not be possible to discuss the findings in detail. However, I will summarize the major empirical findings, arranged according to the main subjects studied.

Rural and Nonmetropolitan Areas

1. Despite rapid outmigration, agriculture is a more important source of employment for blacks in the South than any four manufacturing industries. Blacks were 30

percent of Southern farmers in 1950 and 14 percent in 1969; there were 30 percent as many white farmers in 1969 as in 1950 but only 13 percent as many blacks. In 1969, there were 158,000 nonwhite family farm workers on 84,469 farms; there were 183,638 farms in 1964. Only 24,144 Negro-operated farms in 1969 were in Class I-5 (i.e., with gross sales of $2,500 or more).

2. There were about 250,000 nonwhite paid farm workers in the South in 1969, constituting about one-half of the total hired farm labor force.

3. Fewer white farm operators were farming much more land in 1969 than in 1964; for blacks, land and farms declined. In 1969, the average black farm in the I-5 class was 139 acres, as compared with 400 acres for all farms. The acres operated by Negro farmers declined by 43 percent between 1964 and 1969, as compared with a decline of only 3.6 percent for all farms. Land cultivated by black full owners declined by 14 percent while that operated by white full owners increased by 11 percent; land cultivated by black tenants declined by 70 percent.

4. There has been a shift to off-farm work and income for farm families. Farms with sales less than $5,000 got about three-fourths of their income off the farm. A slightly smaller percentage of blacks reported off-farm work in 1969 as compared with whites, 58 percent and 54 percent respectively.

5. Blacks and many rural whites have not been prepared by education and experience for nonfarm jobs. For blacks males who left Southern agriculture between 1950 and 1969, 80 percent had less than 7 years of education, and 52 percent had less than 4 years. Nevertheless, the

best educated blacks tend to migrate, and their income and employment compare favorably with that of urban-born blacks with similar characteristics. SEO data show the following proportions of blacks 17 years of age and over as high school graduates: migrants, 26 percent; rural residents, 16 percent; urban residents, 39 percent.

6. Manufacturing employment has grown faster in rural than in urban areas, but blacks have not shared proportionately in the gains.

    a. The fastest nonagricultural growth has been outside black population centers.

    b. Even in the population centers, blacks have not shared equitably in the employment gains. Blacks are most underrepresented in white-collar jobs. The greatest black employment gains have been where: manufacturing employment growth is greatest; industry skill requirements are lowest; black work experience is greatest; and black education levels are highest, although this is a weaker factor determining black employment gains than work experience.

    c. Inadequate black employment opportunities in the 244 counties with 5,000 or more blacks in their populations are caused by discrimination on the demand side and the lack of competitive labor market attributes by blacks on the supply side. However, with the data and techniques available to us, we have been unable to resolve the issue of which of these factors is more important.

7. With respect to the future of small farmers, we conclude:

    a. Small farmers have been displaced in part because of the regressive nature of U.S. agricultural policy.

b. With respect to black farmers, there also has been discrimination in the administration of agricultural programs.

c. There are no across-the-board economies of size in agriculture in terms of costs per unit of output. However, technological requirements for optimal-sized farms have increased capital requirements to the point where they are beyond the reach of most poor black farmers in the South.

d. It is conceivable that public policy could reduce significantly the shift of black farmers and farm workers out of agriculture, improve the nonfarm opportunities of rural blacks, and facilitate the movement of blacks who wished to do so from rural to urban areas.

8. Rural manpower programs could play an important role in improving the economic opportunities of blacks, but the potential of these programs is largely unrealized. There is a special problem in extending manpower facilities to rural areas because of the scattered nature of their populations and the paucity of organizations to administer programs. Nevertheless, a number of programs have considerable promise for rural areas, especially programs that relate manpower and economic development, like the "start-up" training concept and Concerted Services in Training and Education (CSTE). Other approaches which seem to have considerable promise include Operation Hitchhike, to extend employment service functions into rural areas, and public employment programs like Operation Mainstream, to provide jobs for

persons not likely to be absorbed into the private sector. Relocation projects also have a limited role to play in a rural manpower strategy.

Metropolitan Employment Patterns

In 1970, for the first time, a majority of Southern blacks lived in metropolitan areas. EEOC data for 1966 and 1969 show:

1. Black females increased their share of metropolitan employment, while the black male share changed very little.

2. Black males increased their share of nonmetropolitan employment, but not as much as black females.

3. Overall, the greatest gains were therefore made in nonmetropolitan areas, although blacks still had a greater share of metropolitan jobs. Moreover, relative to whites, black occupational positions were higher in nonmetropolitan areas than in metropolitan areas.

4. Blacks increased their share of white-collar jobs in metropolitan areas, but remained much more heavily concentrated in the operative, laborer, and service categories than whites.

5. Black women are more evenly represented across occupations than black men, but not across industries. Black women were virtually absent from white-collar jobs in major industries in some Southern SMSA's where larger numbers of white women were employed.

6. These metropolitan-nonmetropolitan employment differences reflect the growth of white-collar jobs in met-

ropolitan areas and blue-collar jobs in nonmetropolitan areas.

The main findings of the city studies (Atlanta, Birmingham, Houston, Louisville, Memphis, Miami, and New Orleans) were as follows:

1. There were general improvements in black political power and more black participation in previously segregated schools and community facilities during the 1960s.

2. Black employment patterns relative to whites apparently did not change very much between the 1920s and the 1960s, but there were noticeable improvements in black income and employment during the last half of the 1960s. Blacks nevertheless remain two or three times as likely as whites to be concentrated in the operative, laborer, and service categories; in 1969, 73 percent of black women and 82 percent of black men were concentrated in these categories.

With respect to government employment, we concluded:

1. Opportunities for blacks were generally superior in government employment to those in the private sector.

2. The highest black penetration rates ordinarily were in local units of government; the lowest were in state governments. The best relative occupational positions were in federal employment.

3. Black employment in state and local government was mainly at the token level, although there were exceptions in every substantial unit of government. The main exceptions to tokenism were in "traditional" jobs historically held by blacks (menial and jobs in segregated institutions) and "new traditional" jobs; the latter are profes-

sional, technical, or nonmenial jobs traditionally closed to blacks but where, as a result of pressure from blacks, a black skin is becoming a requirement.

4. Relative to their proportion of the population, blacks are underrepresented in federal employment in the South and overrepresented in the rest of the country. However, in the South, blacks are overrepresented in Wage Board and underrepresented in General Schedule jobs.

5. In the federal service, there was considerable variation in black employment by agency. Agencies with relatively low black employment were the Departments of Agriculture, Transportation, and Justice and the National Aeronautics and Space Administration, the Internal Revenue Service, the Soil Conservation Service, the Federal Housing Administration, and the Air Force.

6. Departments and agencies with black participation above their proportion of the population (19 percent) were the EEOC (48 percent), OEO (27 percent), GSA (40 percent), Veterans Administration (27 percent), and the Department of Commerce (19 percent).

7. As with private employment, black employment varies inversely with the ratio of white-collar to total employment. As in state and local government, blacks are overrepresented mainly in those agencies with large black client groups.

A regression study of black employment in Southern SMSA's, which attempted to quantify factors reflecting institutional discrimination, used the relative black to white index of occupational position as the dependent variable and the following independent variables: education, age, employment growth rates, geographic area of the SMSA, industry skill levels, and the proportion of nonagricultural employment in manufacturing. The model explained 70 percent of the variance in men's occupational position but only 50 percent for women, indicating, as expected, that the range for possible overt discrimination was much greater for women than for men. All variables except geographic market size were significant for men, but education and the percentage of manufacturing employment were the most powerful positive variables while industry skill requirements was the most important negative variable.

Different variables were associated with female IOP's. The labor market size variable was not important for men but was highly significant for women. The most important explanatory variables for women were concentration relative to whites in ages 20 to 30, market size, economic growth, and relative education above 12 years. As contrasted with their significance in the equation for men, the elementary education and occupational skill requirements variables were not significant for women.

Some of our main conclusions concerning additional causal relationships were:

1. Although there is some controversy regarding the influence of *education* on black employment opportunities, we conclude that education is a significant factor determining black employment patterns, especially for younger blacks who receive more and better education than their elders. Nevertheless, on-the-job training is a more important determinant of black employment opportunity than education.

2. Industry structure is important for males, particu-

larly skill requirements of the industry. This probably explains inadequate black representation in growth industries and those with product market concentration ratios.

3. Transportation was an important factor explaining black participation in low-wage but not high-wage jobs. Since black women are more likely than black men to be in low-wage service jobs, the size of labor markets was a significant determinant of their employment opportunities.

4. Black workers and employers use different labor market information systems for white-collar jobs. The employment service was rarely used by either black workers or employers for white-collar jobs. Moreover, the employment service, with few exceptions, had a very poor image in black communities.

5. Unions were not basic causes of racial employment patterns, but they formalized those patterns through collective bargaining procedures. Craft unions have perpetuated the exclusion of blacks from certain trades, while industrial unions perpetuated job segregation within plants. The racial practices of unions are determined mainly by their structure and the number of blacks in the union or trade. In general, racial discrimination is a membership rather than a leadership problem, so the degree of racial discrimination varies directly with the extent to which unions are controlled by white members.

Conclusions

The evidence supports the conclusion that although

blacks have improved their economic position perceptibly since 1954, the basic patterns are unchanged. However, the process of change accelerated during the last half of the 1960s, after having been relatively stable between the 1920s and the 1960s.

It is tempting to attribute this change to the passage of the Civil Rights Act of 1964, since the fastest changes came after the passage of that act. The Civil Rights Act undoubtedly had something to do with the changes, but careful studies of the enforcement process reveal very limited direct effects on employment. Direct effects are limited because of inadequate enforcement personnel; the fact that legal action is expensive, time consuming, and uncertain as to outcome; and the fact that antidiscrimination measures ordinarily operate to influence the demand side of the employment equation but do very little to influence the supply of qualified people to take advantage of the opportunities opened up.

If the Civil Rights Act had an impact on black employment in the South, it probably was due mainly to its general moral impact to cause "voluntary" compliance rather than to the effects of legal enforcement of the act.

However, there were other forces for change, including the broad economic and social changes mentioned earlier. These forces set the trends, but organized pressures from blacks provided the impetus for change. Our studies suggest that the greatest changes in black employment ordinarily come about where there is organized pressure from blacks and whites who share their objectives.

Technological changes have had important influences

on black employment by displacing blacks from some jobs, particularly in agriculture, but increasing the skill requirements of industry.

Tight labor markets improve black employment opportunities by increasing the demand for workers and overcoming white workers' job control motives for not hiring blacks. At the same time, tight labor markets increase the employers' profit motive for hiring blacks, since whites generally will be in shorter supply. It should be emphasized, however, that tight labor markets are not sufficient causes of change, because there are many tight labor markets in Southern cities where employment change has been very gradual indeed.

The most significant factor other than increased demand for labor is increased supplies, which, as we have argued, are a significant factor influencing the power of blacks to break down resistance from white workers. Supplies have been increased through improvements in black education levels and manpower programs. But job segregation has denied blacks access to on-the-job training, which is one of the main ways people acquire skills. Desegregation of jobs therefore has increased blacks' ability to acquire this important source of training.

I would like to conclude with an observation on the process through which racial discrimination and attitudes interact with the forces of change. If we start with institutionalized discrimination such as existed in the South around 1900, we noted many general forces associated with industrialization tending to erode discrimination. However, these forces are not automatic and require conscious decision in particular places in order for change to take place. Changing circumstances tend to change racial attitudes, reducing the bias that accounts for discrimination. Attitudes apparently change as blacks are included in nontraditional jobs because of a tendency by whites to rationalize behavior they are forced by circumstances to take, or which they wish to take. In short, strategies to change black status and employment work together in the long run to reduce bias and discrimination.

Comments by JAMES M. STEPP

Shortly after finishing high school in 1929, I began four years of experience as a factory worker, retail clerk, job hunter and (with my father) tenant farmer in one of North Carolina's low-income western counties; and when I finished college in 1937 I received only one rather unattractive job offer. My personal interest in improving economic opportunities for residents of low-income rural areas merged into an active professional interest that has existed ever since I joined the faculty of Clemson University in 1940. I have had no professional interest in the "race problem" as such; I have generally viewed the most objectional aspects of "racism" as side effects of the poverty problem. While I was a boy my father was a retail grocer with both black and white customers, and I delivered groceries to both. I learned early in life that honest people who have good jobs make the best customers regardless of the color of their skins.

In preparing for this program, I reviewed some of my writings in the 1940s to see what, if anything, I had to say about the economic status and opportunities of Negroes. In 1944 I had directed a community postwar planning

47

study of up-country Anderson, South Carolina, and in 1945 a similar study of low-country Sumter, South Carolina.

Among other things, we were interested in prospective incomes, purchasing power, and the balance between prospective labor supply and prospective jobs. At that time, there were still some fairly clear-cut racial patterns of employment (especially in textile manufacturing), and employers had not yet become afraid to state their preferences regarding race and sex of their work force; hence I used the race and sex as the basis for some of my tabulations. One such tabulation was 1940 occupations in each of the two cities. Considering their locations, the data for Negroes were remarkably similar: Negro men: 43 percent nonfarm laborers in Sumter, and 31 percent in Anderson; 38 percent craftsmen and operators in Sumter, and 37 percent in Anderson—Negro women: 85 percent domestic and other services in Sumter, and 91 percent in Anderson.

While the labor shortage generated by World War II changed some racial patterns of employment, the beneficial income effects did not spread very widely throughout the black community. For example, in 1944 I said:

This survey does provide fairly accurate data as to family incomes in Greater Anderson for the year 1943.

The most striking feature about these data on incomes is the high percentage of white families and the low percentage of the Negro families with relatively large incomes and, conversely, the low percentage of white families and the high percentage of Negro families with distressingly small incomes.

Those of us who were trying to persuade the "estab-

lishment" to provide better opportunities for Negroes
were, in retrospect, not very forceful. Having (in 1944)
discovered a potential postwar unemployment problem
in Anderson unless more jobs were created, I went on to
say:

Finally, it is to be noted that the prosperity of the mercantile
and service establishments of the city and county would be
greatly increased if some way could be devised to provide more
productive work and higher incomes for Negroes. The same
thing is true of course, with respect to better jobs for white
workers with extremely low incomes, but they are not nearly so
numerous as the low-paid Negro workers. People with low
incomes have so many unsatisfied wants that when they get
extra money they spend most of it immediately. Some special
training for people of low skills would no doubt yield excellent
business and civic dividends.

Incidentally, South Carolina has pioneered in establishing a statewide system of technical education centers
which work closely with new industries to train their
workers, and it has for nearly two decades been yielding
excellent business and civic dividends.

Rationale for Rural Development

By the mid-1940s I had become convinced that the only
way to "solve" the poverty problem and to alleviate the
race problem in the South was to make a systematic effort
to provide industrial jobs in small towns and rural areas.
Since then some of my colleagues and I at Clemson University and at other institutions in other states have been

working constantly toward that end through federal, state, local, and private development agencies.

My economic rationale for promoting rural (and small-town) industrial development and opposing migration to urban areas was presented at some length at a Washington, D.C., meeting in February 1948. Since much of what I said 25 years ago is still valid for many parts of the South, I shall repeat a few excerpts from that paper:

The forgotten people of American agriculture are the low-income farm families. It is a well-known fact, which requires no documentation here, that on about half of the farms of the nation annual production is so low that there is no feasible or probable agricultural price level that will provide a decent level of living for the operators of such farms. It is also well known that the South has far more than its proportionate share of farms of this type. . . .

Except for a few programs of limited coverage, neither the Federal nor the State agricultural agencies devote much time or expense to activities aimed specifically toward the improvement of the economic status of the most disadvantaged half of our farmers. Furthermore, there is all too prevalent a tendency to class farm wage workers along with mules, machinery and fertilizer as simply cost items, and to rejoice when wage costs are low and complain when they are high. . . .

There is, of course, no single cause of the predominance of low incomes in southern agriculture. It is generally known that the South contains too many farm people in proportion to its available land and capital. On the other hand, however, all students of southern agriculture know that the most efficient use is not made of the land and capital that are available. Having said all of this, however, it must be admitted that the most fundamental cause of low farm incomes in the South is not to be found in how our farms are managed or mismanaged. The solution to this problem must be sought outside of rather than within agriculture. . . .

There is every reason to believe that industrial development in rural areas of the South offers much better opportunities for improving the economic status of the region than either migration of population out of the South or direct improvements in the efficiency of southern agriculture. As a matter of fact, if good alternative employment opportunities are not readily available to southern farm people, the outlook for large increases in the efficiency of southern agricultural labor is exceedingly dim. . . .

For a variety of economic, social and psychological reasons, most people will move a short distance to accept a new job much more readily than they will move a long distance. . . .

It follows that, other things being equal, the economic interests of the South will be better served by establishing industrial plants in low-income rural areas than by establishing them either in other parts of the nation or in a few large southern cities. Some of the major impediments to shifting from agricultural to nonagricultural occupations will not be present if the employment opportunities are in nearby industrial establishments. The workers in such industries do not necessarily have to move into towns. . . .

While some interregional migration is undoubtedly desirable, the best interests of the South will not be served by having all of its surplus farm workers move to other parts of the nation. It has been pointed out by numerous writers that any region suffers a social and economic loss if it experiences a continuous net out-migration of adult population. . . .

Even though young people growing up in low-income families do not enjoy a high level of living and do not as a rule have an opportunity to obtain a great deal of education, there is considerable cost involved in rearing and educating them. This cost is not recovered by the South if young southern adults move to other parts of the nation to spend the productive years of their lives and pay their taxes. . . .

There is a great deal of competition among states and among localities within states for industrial plants, and for a particular locality to be successful its leaders must present its advantages fully and forcefully. . . . This places small agriculturally-based towns at a distinct disadvantage. The civic leaders and officials in such towns rarely know what sort of data are pertinent, where to obtain the proper information, or how to relate such information to the question of industrial location. Economists in the South might well concern themselves with those questions and be prepared to render assistance along those lines.

Changes in South Carolina

During the past 25 years South Carolina (as well as North Carolina) has developed along the lines I was advocating. We have experienced rapid industrial growth that is fairly widely dispersed throughout most of the state; almost everyone lives within comfortable commuting distance of one or more new manufacturing plants. However, until about 10 years ago blacks failed to get a reasonable share of these new jobs because many of the new jobs were in the state's only truly segregated industry—textile manufacturing. This logjam was, of course, broken by political action in the mid-1960s. Since then the political pressure for "Affirmative Action" and the economic pressure of labor shortages and high-wage industrial competitors has caused the textile industry to recruit black workers so vigorously that it has become the dominant employer of both black men and black women. During the past 20 years the textile manufacturing industry has been moving into the Carolinas and Georgia (from 38 percent of the national total in 1950 to 56 percent in 1970), and since 1960 black workers of both sexes have been rapidly moving into the textile plants of this area. If they follow the pattern of their "hillbilly" and "red-neck" predecessors, they will move up in the textile industry and out into other higher-paying industries.

The University of South Carolina Bureau of Business and Economic Research is in the process of completing a detailed study of changes in employment in South Carolina between 1960 and 1970, and they have let me have a copy of the current draft of the report. The most striking changes were (a) the drastic reduction in agricultural employment of both races; two-thirds for blacks and one-half for whites; (b) the doubling of the number and percentage of blacks employed in manufacturing, while the number of whites increased by only 17 percent and the percentage of white workers employed in manufacturing declined by about 10 percent.

The percentage of black men employed in manufacturing rose from 23.4 in 1960 to 34.5 in 1970, and the percentage of employed black women holding manufacturing jobs in South Carolina rose from only 4 in 1960 to 23 in 1970. During the 1960s the number of manufacturing jobs held by blacks in this state increased by 34,522, of which 20,830 were held by women. Almost half (48.2 percent) of the state's 10-year growth in manufacturing employment was accounted for by blacks, who comprise (in 1970) only 30.4 percent of the total population and 26.3 percent of the labor force. In the textile industry, the number of white workers declined somewhat, but the decline was more than offset by the large increase in the number of black textile workers. However, since they started so late, the proportion of blacks in the textile industry (18.2 percent of all employees in 1970) is still considerably lower than their relative strength in the state's labor force (26.3 percent).

To summarize, the past decade has seen a peaceful economic revolution in South Carolina. The percentage of the labor force employed on farms has for the first time dropped to the national average (less than 4 percent). For the first time in our 300-year history as a colony and as a state, our black citizens are participating fully, if not yet proportionally, in the benefits of economic growth and improvement. During the 1960s some 60,000 of them shifted from low-paid agricultural and personal services jobs into manufacturing, trade, professional and related services, and other activities. The greatest impact of this economic revolution has been felt by black women, who have only within the past decade achieved something close to full economic citizenship in South Carolina. The trend is very good, and the situation will be better in the future.

III

Southern Literature:

The Last Twenty Years

WALTER SULLIVAN

THE RELATIONSHIP between the literary artist and the society in which he lives is very mysterious, and I do not claim to know much about it. This is, you will immediately perceive, a very poor way for me to begin, but I want to be honest with you and I need once more to remind myself of the dangers of oversimplification. For example, one way of addressing the question I have been assigned to discuss—what has happened to Southern literature since 1954—would be to say that it has declined grieviously and to give evidence, which is readily available, of that decline. Such an approach would put me on the safest possible ground: no one believes that William Styron is as good as William Faulkner and Faulkner was finished with his best work before the decision in *Brown v. Board of Education* was rendered. No recent poets are as good as Tate and Ransom, and so I could go on comparing the major figures of the Southern literary renascence to writers who have emerged since World War II to the distinct disadvantage of the latter.

But you know all this already, and what you and I want to discover is why the literature of the 1950s and 1960s is not as good as that of the 1920s and 1930s. More specifically still, we want to know how social changes have affected the literature of the South and ultimately what the court decision did to shape the literature of this section. The last question is easiest, so let me try to answer that first: I suspect that the decision per se had a most negligible effect on the course of Southern letters. The decision, after all, is simply an image, a point of definition, a palpable historical fact that at once stood for the vast changes that had been made in the South and adumbrated the many problems that remained to be dealt with. From a literary point of view, I suspect we might just as well use as our image that moment in December 1955 when Mrs. Rosa Parks refused to move to the back of the bus in Montgomery or any one of the lunch counter sit-ins at various cities in the South. In other words, when I speak of the society in which the Southern writer lives and works, I am thinking of the whole complex of history and event and social and moral and even metaphysical climate that issue into moments of definition such as the one we are examining at this conference. So this, as I conceive it, is my task: to talk about Southern society in its relationship to Southern literature over the last several years.

But first, I must go back. The Southern literary rena-
scence came to fruition between the two World Wars.
Faulkner was its giant, but there were many others, all of
whom had lived their formative years in the South before
1917: Thomas Wolfe, Allen Tate, John Crowe Ransom,
Andrew Lytle, Caroline Gordon, Katherine Anne Porter,
Robert Penn Warren, Donald Davidson. The list could be
expanded in almost any direction: Erskine Caldwell;
Stark Young; John Gould Fletcher; William Alexander
Percy; Eudora Welty, who was born in 1909; and Ellen
Glasgow, who was born in 1874, but who lived until 1945
and wrote many of her best novels in the 1920s and 1930s.
The high level of accomplishment achieved by these
Southern writers and their contemporaries is beyond
question. Lewis Simpson remarks that the Fugitive-
Agrarians in Nashville were the "most intense and coher-
ent literary group in America since the Transcenden-
talists." Tate and Ransom are among our very best poets;
Cleanth Brooks is one of our very best critics. Yet, with
few exceptions, the renascence died before the men and
women who created it.

The example of Faulkner is extravagant, but it is typical
enough. Between 1929 and 1942, Faulkner created what
we have come to call his myth of the South. Simply to
repeat the titles of the novels he wrote during this period
is to recapitulate one of the most brilliant and prolific
literary careers of this century. *Sartoris, The Sound and
the Fury, Sanctuary, As I Lay Dying, Absalom, Absalom!,
The Unvanquished, The Hamlet, Go Down Moses*, which
is not to name them all. Then, in 1948, he published
Intruder in the Dust, and the diminution of his talents

was apparent. *A Fable* and *The Mansion* were painfully egregious performances; *The Town* and *The Reivers* were pale shadows of what Faulkner had been able to do in his prime. Most of the best writers of the renascence suffered the same fate. Katherine Anne Porter's long-awaited novel *Ship of Fools* was a distinct disappointment. Warren published *All the King's Men* in 1946 and then fell into a decline. What I wish to emphasize is that a sudden reversal in form by a single author is of no significance. Individual careers vary and individual writers discover their own most productive years. But when an entire literary movement fails while the people who produced that movement go on living and working, it seems logical to deduce that something in the background, some aspect of the social or historical or moral situation has changed sufficiently to deprive the writers of whatever it is they need to write well.

Scholars are agreed on the cultural factors which made the Southern renascence possible. The people in the South were a homogeneous lot: pious, agrarian in their orientation, inheritors of a generation which had lost the Civil War and suffered through the poverty that followed. As readers of the King James Version of the Bible, Southerners were trained in the very best use of the English language. Perhaps as a result of this—for good writing is always precise—and of the example set by Christ's habitual use of parables, Southerners developed an instinct for narrative, which is, in the final analysis an instinct for the concrete. Unlike their brethren in the North, they put scant faith in abstract theory. Still, even if we concede that all these conditions obtained, why did

the renascence not come, say, in 1890 rather than in 1920?
Because before 1920, the South was still too much the
South. In a traditional culture, a literary renascence is
most likely to occur when social and political and religious
institutions begin to alter and decay. As Donald Davidson
has pointed out, the phenomenon can be observed in
Greece during the fifth century B.C., in Rome in the days
of the late republic, in England during the sixteenth
century. "With the War of 1914–1918," says Allen Tate,
"The South re-entered the modern world—but gave a
backward glance as it stepped over the border; that backward glance gave us the Southern renascence, a literature
conscious of the past in the present."

With this much as background—though I must warn
you that I am not yet quite finished with the past—I
should like to enlarge the question to which I was asked to
address myself. Keeping in mind that the Supreme Court
decision of 1954 is an image of the revised status of the
black man in Southern society, it seems proper to inquire
what role blacks played in creating the cultural conditions
conducive to the renascence and what bearing their present condition has on the literary situation.

I would not presume to tell this audience what the
experience of the black man was in the South before
World War II. Almost all of you have examined this
actuality more closely than I. But how does he appear in
the novels of the 1920s, 1930s, and early 1940s? In the first
place, his role is remarkably ambiguous. Except in very
rare instances, he is not a major figure, yet he is always
there and his presence is felt. As Elizabeth Spencer put it
in a novel of later vintage, his voice is continually heard at

the back door. Frequently, but by no means always, he is
a stock character. He is a servant or menial because no
other role is open to him. He may be old, wise, respected,
and loved by the white people he has spent his life serving
and to whom he is devoted. He may be young and lazy or
middle aged and wicked, or he may simply exist, speaking
his lines and doing what is required of him, driving the
carriage or working in the garden, or cleaning the house.
He did not, Allen Tate reminds us, make a proper peasant
but he was a member of a lower class and his oppression
must have contributed to the maintenance of a class-
conscious society in the South. In a way, this is what the
literature of the renascence is all about: community and
class.

Malcolm Cowley tells us that with a little cleverness we
could see Faulkner's entire Yoknapatawpha cycle of
novels as a legend of the defeat of the aristocratic South.
People such as the Compsons and Sartorises struggled to
preserve a way of life which was based on a code of
behavior and attitude: first against the Union Army and
the carpetbaggers who followed them; then against the
Snopeses, the new breed of white Southerners who out
Yankeed the Yankees in their disregard of social amenities
and their contempt for ethical behavior. The Snopeses
were destined to win even if they lost, for the only way to
defeat a Snopes is to become more of one than he is. But
through this conflict, which culminates in the destruction
of the old Southern culture, what becomes of the black
man? He is out of the frying pan and into the fire; he gains
nothing. If anything, the Snopeses are more careless of his
welfare and more determined to oppress him than his

aristocratic masters were. And in the bargain, he has lost whatever small benefits derived from the humble position he occupied in the previously well-defined class structure. Thus the matter stood in 1940. The subsequent social upheaval that accompanied the war made the victory of the Snopeses complete.

You will understand that I am speaking in terms of hegemonies: nothing is as absolute or as simple as I am presenting it here, but by 1945 there was not enough of the old culture left to keep the images that had served the writers of the renascence alive. Yoknapatawpha County, the red-necks who voted for Willie Stark, the slightly rundown Texas aristocrats who worshiped the memory of Amy in "Old Mortality" were no longer viable as literary properties. This was true because the dramatic tensions within the culture had changed. The old struggle had ended; a new one was to begin; and at the center of the new conflict out of which, like it or not, Southern literature would have to be written was the black man. Faulkner understood this and his response to the new conditions was to write *Intruder in the Dust*, but fiction is action, not debate, and Faulkner was unable to solve the dramatic problems that faced him under the new dispensation.

Faulkner was not, is not, alone. The truth is—and I want to state the matter unequivocally—the new theme is vastly inferior to the old. One reason for this is that essential to the creation of literature is a strong sense of the flawed nature of mankind. Literature is about the human condition: it tells us about ourselves; it shows us the consequences of our humanity. But it must begin always with the fundamental truth and the truth is that we are all imperfect. Now, in the South in the first four decades of this century, the imperfections of individuals as well as the imperfections of the culture were easy enough to spot. In actual fact, life in the South may not have been any more unjust than life in other sections of the country, and certainly, there was less oppression and less misery in the South than existed in most other sections of the world. But because of the presence of the black man—and this is one of the great contributions he made to the renascence—the common guilt was obvious and palpable. There was no way for a Southerner to delude himself into thinking that man was perfect or even perfectible as long as he had to conduct his affairs in the presence of an oppressed minority every single day.

Or let me put the matter this way: the conflict between the Sartorises and the Snopeses was—like all human conflicts—a struggle between two imperfections. It is true that the victorious Snopeses were on balance worse than the aristocrats, but the aristocrats were deeply flawed by sin. The authors of the renascence grasped this verity, found the images in their society to express it, and therefore showed us more clearly what we ourselves are. But when the remnant of the defeated aristocrats and the victorious Snopeses make common cause against the aspirations of the black man, the literary background, the conditions for artistic creation are greatly changed. Instead of a basic conflict between two sides composed of morally complicated human beings, we have one side composed of the virtuous and the other side made up of the sinful—the good guys and the bad. However the causes may be adjudicated, to see life and the people who live it in this fashion is to see a lie.

In a recent book called *The Death of Art,* Floyd Watkins gives us the results of a wide study he has made of recent Southern novels and confirms what we already suspected. Almost invariably, the black characters are virtuous, handsome, in every way heroic; the white characters are also virtuous, handsome, in every way heroic, *if they have fully embraced the cause of equal rights.* Otherwise, they are dishonest, ugly, and in every way reprehensible. In other words, right and wrong, good and evil, wisdom and stupidity, all morally qualitative standards have been reduced to one single measurement: where does one stand on the question of civil rights? To see life in such abecedarian terms is to reduce it; and, as Watkins' title suggests, for the artist the reduced vision is the way to death. In support of this thesis, let me point you to an example. Tolstoy, one of the greatest of all novelists, was a superb creator of characters. Even the bit players in his books come to life with all the complexity and angularity of real human beings. Yet, his portrait of Napoleon in *War and Peace* is flat, dead, and totally unconvincing. He hated the Frenchman too much to grant him his virtues.

If we approach this problem from another direction, we discover that the modern Southern novelist has forgotten what he should know about his art. A primary rule of the craft, lucidly enunciated by Conrad in a famous essay, is that the writer works from the concrete to the abstract. He renders exactly the specific details of sight and sound and action. He must be first of all accurate in depicting the surface of the world. He must not start at the other end, with the abstraction, which is another way of saying, he must not begin with a preconception. An author does not write because he knows all the answers inherent in his subject. He writes because he has an overwhelming desire to discover the truth about his material. The truth that he unearths will depend in part on his own beliefs and his own temperament, but he must find the abstract principle by the process of rendering the concrete honestly. He must find out what he thinks and who he is, and if he is to be successful, he must sooner or later catch himself unawares. No surprise for the writer, no surprise for the reader, said Robert Frost, and almost every other writer in history has echoed this statement.

Finally, think of this question in terms of intellectual conformity. The artist must live in a state of tension with his society. If he simply glorifies his own culture, refusing to see its faults, he fails. If he sees nothing but its evil and loses all affection for it, he fails. The modern Southern writer finds himself in a peculiar situation. He must endure in a divided community and this is bad enough for his work. But so all pervading is the struggle for black equality that he must sooner or later participate in it, which means he must take sides. As a civilized man, he takes the side of the blacks and relinquishes his own freedom. The answers which he ought to be seeking in his art have already been found and the artist knows what they are. His attitudes have already been defined for him. He can only reiterate what he knows, create his characters to fit preconceived molds and endow them with a bare minimum of liberty. The result is unsatisfactory to say the least.

I must tell you that in my own small way, I too once had a dream of a future better than the present. Like the teacher of languages in Conrad's *Under Western Eyes,* I thought that the future would be kind to us all, not in terms of our human relationships, though I desire to see these improved, but in terms of our literature. Surely, the times we have been living through since the court decision of 1954 have been fraught with meaning and excitement and drama. I hoped that some day, some writer, not of my generation but of a generation to come, would probe the events that we have lived through and thereby help to explain our history to us I am thinking of someone who would be sufficiently divorced from the inflamed passions that have necessarily been generated by the agonies that we have undergone and continue to endure; someone who would stand in the same relation to the present conflict that Faulkner assumed in relation to the Snopes-Sartoris confrontation; someone who would know, as Shakespeare's Henry V points out that "there is no king, be his cause never so spotless, if it come to the arbitrament of swords, can try it out with all unspotted soldiers."

Though the comparison may seem to you inept, the modern novelist approaching the fictional material that is inherent in the search for racial justice, is in the position in which Bell Irvin Wiley found himself when he tried to research the sex habits of Confederate soldiers. Since he was doing his work some years ago, he could find veterans enough to question. But they all fed him the same line. Why, they said, Confederate soldiers would never do such things. We know, if not from personal experience, then from what all of literature from the beginning until now has taught us, that inside the great forces that we have watched at work, within the great organizations that have brightened our history for the last twenty years by their successful efforts to bring justice to the black man—inherent in this cause, because it is a human cause, is human perfidy. On the great marches, in the councils of the NAACP, in CORE and SNCC, and the other organizations, there must have been bad people along with the good, doubters along with the faithful, self-seekers along with those who offered themselves completely. This has to be the truth, because the black man is a human being. And he must be portrayed in literature as such—which means that like Hamlet and Anna Karenina and Tom Jones and Don Quixote he must be allowed his share of weakness and evil. My dream was—and I still dare somewhat to cherish it—that some as yet undiscovered writer would create some black villains and thereby restore to the black man in general the dignity he deserves.

I am aware that I have flagrantly begged the question I was supposed to answer. I have told you that the literature of the last twenty years is inferior to that of the renascence and I have tried to show you the conditions and attitudes that make it inferior, but concerning the literature itself I have told you very little. But in this matter you do not need my help. Read *Absalom, Absalom!* and compare it to William Styron's *The Confessions of Nat Turner;* read Eudora Welty's *The Golden Apples* and then Madison Jones' *A Cry of Absence;* read the poems of John Ransom and those of James Dickey. You will see what I mean.

Comments by ALFRED S. REID

Mr. Sullivan has just said—if he will permit me to reduce his paper to two points—that Southern literature since 1954 has been so poor in quality, compared with the writing of the preceding years, that the cause of civil rights, symbolized by the 1954 desegregation decision, could not help being "negligible." The decline had set in before 1950. Since then, there has been no novelist of the stature of Faulkner, no poet of the stature of Ransom and Tate. If the Supreme Court decision has had any effect, he goes on to say, it has contributed to this decline in quality because it has encouraged the creation of over-simplified characters—either all good or all bad—and because it encourages a simple worldview based on social justice instead of a complex worldview based on original sin.

For the sake of argument, I shall disagree in some measure with Mr. Sullivan's thesis. Momentarily, let me hold off any comment on the first half of this proposition, the decline in quality, and comment first on two significant literary developments occasioned by the civil rights movement. The first is the opening up of new possibilities for interpreting Negro character. For more than a hundred years, the Negro appeared in Southern writing in subhuman stereotypes. As Mr. Sullivan said, he was a servant or menial. He was usually a shallow comic figure, a shuffling, dancing, laughing, cotton-picking coon or minstrel. Or he was the faithful servant, the deferential darky who reflected his master's feelings but had no feelings of his own. Or he was the villain-rapist-murderer, the incorrigible nigger, the bogeyman of society. Or he was the pathetic freeman, attached to neither whites nor blacks, a forlorn outcast. We find variations of these types in Faulkner—in the comic ne'er-do-well Percival Brownlee, in the loyal black mammy Dilsey, and in the outcast rapist-murderer Joe Christmas. Faulkner's most individualized Negro is probably that stubborn, self-willed tenant-farmer Lucas Beauchamp. Perhaps as Floyd Watkins says in *The Death of Art*, there has been a tendency to reverse the stereotypes in recent years and make the black man all-virtuous. Although I have not read all the novels that Floyd Watkins and Walter Sullivan have read, I am inclined to think that the expansion of black characters into more diversified human roles is a trend in the right direction. We see blacks now not as mere menial or comic reflections of white characters but as middle-class entrepreneurs, school principals, band directors, factory foremen, sheriffs, preachers, and militant civil rights advocates. The most ambitious literary performance is, of course, William Styron's *The Confessions of Nat Turner*, an exhaustive analysis of feelings and motivations that show a flawed human being's capacity for good and evil, success and failure. More writers, in other words, are attributing to blacks the status of individualized manhood, and I think this trend is all to the good in Southern letters.

The second significant development is the emergence of the black writer. Limited before World War II by lack of education and other opportunities, Southern blacks rarely broke into print. The most notable exception is Richard Wright. More recently, Southern blacks have joined in the renascence of an Afro-American literature of genuine passion for justice in the liberal democratic tradition of Jefferson, Emerson, Thoreau, Whitman, and Lincoln—a passion heretofore conspicuously absent in Southern writing after John C. Calhoun. As Mr. Sullivan says, Southern writing, even at its best, has been concerned with an aristocratic class-consciousness doomed from within by its complex evils and from without by the emergence of the Snopeses and other lesser breeds. Perhaps, after all, the great image in Southern letters since Faulkner is precisely that of the black man suffering humiliation nonviolently and going off to jail rather than obey laws he considers unjust. The image appears at its sharpest, of course, in Martin Luther King's "Letter from a Birmingham Jail," *Stride Toward Freedom,* and in the surprising oration "I Have a Dream" delivered on the steps of the Lincoln Memorial during the March on Washington in 1963. In these essays we find ringing declarations of freedom and justice, arresting figures of speech, rolling periods, telling aphorisms and antitheses—a style reminiscent of Amos and Isaiah. Here are significant expressions of courage and prophecy, of love and long suffering. Here are moving expressions of that sense of "nobodiness," of exile and alienation, that have come to be typical of twentieth-century literature. A trend that has given us this image and style is, I think, a commendable one.

When we return now to Mr. Sullivan's other main point—that Southern literature has fallen into an abysmal decline—I cannot play the devil's advocate as easily. Nearly everyone agrees that there has been a falling off. I would, however, make a few observations to help, if possible, put this decline into perspective. First, there has been a national decline—all the so-called moderns are gone, and there have been no comparable replacements. To attribute the Southern decline to the rise of a liberal stance does indeed beg the question. Second, I cannot accept the implication that all recent Southern writers are inferior to all writers of the 1920s. I realize Mr. Sullivan has not made precisely that point, but generalizations of this sort have a way of becoming twisted. Styron is not the equal of Faulkner or Wolfe or Warren in Warren's one good novel, but *Nat Turner* certainly beats anything by Caldwell, Gordon, and Young, and might just be grander than anything by Porter and Welty. James Dickey is not as sharp as Ransom or as Tate in Tate's one great poem, but Dickey is probably better as a poet, I would say, than Warren as a poet and better in more poems than Tate is. Third, this whole exercise of setting up kingpins misses another point, and that is that recent achievements need examination on their own terms. We have just recently learned to interpret Faulkner and his contemporaries. We now need to interpret the new people whose works are different because their world is different. James Dickey, for instance, gives us a vision of our time—a sense of guilt about bombing innocent people, a lust for life and virility, a need for transcending self. William Jay Smith, though not a Ransom or Tate, gives a grace and joy. And if literature is the focusing of experience in an image of meaningful intensity, then King, as I have said, has given to Southern letters, without claiming to be a literary figure, a commendable clarity. He has renewed the Southern conscience and salvaged it from the stranglehold that rendered even Bayard Sartoris and Isaac McCaslin morally impotent and ruined Faulkner's *Intruder in the Dust*. We cannot deny that there are no overpowering figures now, but there is a range and richness, and often fervor, that we need to recognize among the many minor voices, white and black, who have written during a significant time for social justice in Southern history.

IV

Reform, Change, and Irony

ERNEST Q. CAMPBELL

L ET ME TRY to make my perspective clear in the beginning of these remarks: There has been an important social revolution in our Southland in the last two decades, and there is no retreating from its major contours. We are set on a course of reduced racial barriers and increased public contact. I understand those who believe that the pace of change has not been rapid enough, whose hurt hurts and whose future fades, but I insist that we not disparage the mammoth realignments that have occurred. The state is no longer the conscious instrument of those who wish to oppress, to set one race above another. Many of the changes are specific and tangible: there are no more segregated waiting rooms and separate drinking fountains; blacks vote and hold public office; the races sit side by side in the public schools and universities of the region—the multiple forms of microsegregation which constituted a distinctive social order are no more. Indeed, an entire new generation has grown up who can hardly believe that it ever happened and to whom it reads like ancient history. Read again Bertram W. Doyle's *The Etiquette of Race Relations in the South* if you cannot believe it was real or if your memory is dim.

It is not only that Jim Crow is dead; we have seen changes in intangibles that are fully as substantial. The styles of deference are gone; where whites once welcomed the chance to use ironically the honorific titles "Reverend," "Doctor," and "Professor" to avoid the simpler recognition, "Mister," now common forms of respectful address are customary. Foot-shuffling styles and the Sambo mentality are today unacceptable to blacks and by and large unexpected by whites. Blacks have become an articulate interest group in community processes, sometimes getting what they want, often not, but presenting their demands in a style shockingly forthright by the standards we knew a mere handful of years ago; the "uppitty nigger" of 1950 is an Uncle Tom by comparison. Protest is legitimate, and in most areas of the region those who threaten boycotts, marches, and political reprisal sleep without fear at night, their activities having become as routinely accepted as those of a lawyer who defends his client in court. Certain blacks may still play Brer Fox and Brer Rabbit games, but these are increasingly tactical choices and not forced necessities. The white community has lost its capacity to maneuver the allocation of small favors in such manner as effectively designates the spokesmen and leaders for the black community. Harsh realities remain among us, but the growth of a mature autonomy among Southern blacks must be acknowledged as an awesome modification in the region's social structure.

It was not our good will and robust warm nature, but agitation, pressure, and federal power that brought this about. These are not accomplishments, they are compliances. But they seem natural to us now and there is no turning back.

Commentaries

I am not confident that these next remarks are appropriate to the theme of this conference. Yet I think they touch upon things that have emerged into our awareness during the past two decades and I would argue that they are more substantial than they seem. I want to present six mini-essays, capsule commentaries if you will, which I believe deserve our reflection.

VIGNETTE ONE

Those who have struggled to reform the South, including many distinguished native sons and daughters, have typically used the nation as a proper model. Who among us has not heard such exhortations as "let's join the nation," . . . "get into the mainstream of American life,"

. . . "catch up with the twentieth century," . . . "quit being so backward?" An interesting thing happened: beseeched to get into the mainstream, we entered it, and when we got in—it was polluted. Dick Gregory once joked that he sat-in at a lunch counter for six months and when they finally agreed to feed him they didn't have what he wanted. But there was a serious meaning beneath his joke, and I too wish to be taken seriously: the South has become more a part of the nation at just the time that national longings have turned toward virtues long associated with the South (at least in myth)—nature, land hunger, simplicity, rootedness, stability, family, small town, intimacy. Reacting to the awful complexities and tensions of industrial cities and technological management, to polluted air and water, traffic jams, and letters typed by computer, vast numbers of Americans, their chorus swelled by the youth movements of the 1960s, have felt warranted to ask, with the singer close to suicide, "Is That All There Is?"

A distinguished and eloquent South Carolinian, James McBride Dabbs, published a book called *The Southern Heritage* in 1958. He called on the region, it seemed to me, to return to its heritage and work out its problems within the framework of the styles it knew best and ought to preserve. Some might call Mr. Dabbs a romantic dreamer, a spokesman for traditions that never were. I would not. I think there is reason to believe that there can grow from this region's heritage the fullest realization this nation will have of the unproven, experimental notion that justice and good will can obtain in a multiracial society.

VIGNETTE TWO

It is worthy of note that during these past twenty years the white man has had the shocking experience of *rejection* by blacks. Whatever the tensions and the bitterness, he has always been comfortably assured that he was the model for the black man. "Look at that darky," he might say, "doing his darnedest to act like a white man, and he doesn't know how." And he might add in disgust (and fear) "What they want is to come into our homes and churches, eat at our tables, and marry our daughters." Whether this was *ever* literally true is beside the point; whites believed it to be true and no one contradicted them. And then came the stunning accomplishments of the black pride movement. "We've seen your churches and God is not there, the place is too cold for Him." . . . "Marry your daughters? It's you who've been obsessed with us, not we with you. Black is beautiful." . . . "Eat at your tables? There's no soul food there." Extremists have indeed called for literal separation into a "Black Nation," but the more substantial black voices said instead that the black community would provide its own heroes, its own leaders, its own institutions, its own ambitions, and its own sources of pride.

I do not think that black separatism can get very far or runs very deep; blacks *really are* too much like other Americans. But it may take a long time for "whitey" to adjust to the shock of this rejection.

VIGNETTE THREE

One of the dilemmas black citizens face—and in its way it is a tragedy—is that history gives them bountiful reason to distrust the leadership of whites. It would be an act of extraordinary generosity (even of foolhardiness) for blacks willingly to leave their fate in the hands of whites. Their rights of citizenship would erode as surely as iron rusts. Yet blacks are, in most places, a numerical minority. Most of the decision makers in most places are certain to be whites, and as blacks merge into the institutional framework—if only to watch over the shoulders of whites to protect black rights—the less distinctive they become and the less they sustain the nurturing community that offers solace and soothing warmth. Herewith the common dilemma of the minority: the more withdrawn, the more authentic—yet the more vulnerable; the more involved, the more effective advocacy—yet the greater internal dissolution. This is not necessarily a no-win situation —witness the case of Jews in the United States—but it is a troublesome companion of emerging rights and opportunities for blacks. I shall say more on this matter later.

VIGNETTE FOUR

I want to note in passing the distinctive analogies between traditional white stereotypes of blacks and some important contemporary movements and themes in American life. Let me mention a few. Here is a stereotype: "Blacks are lazy; they don't work, they like to laze around and rap with each other." Here's a modern, highly legitimate theme: "You only go round once. The rat race is deadly; man wasn't made to punch a clock. Enjoy youself; press yourself and you have a heart attack. Learn to use leisure and prepare for more of it." Or, here is another stereotype: "Blacks are sensuous, sexual, loose, expressive, happy-go-lucky." And here is another contemporary theme: "Express yourself in dance and story. Don't be so uptight; get over your hang-ups. What's so sinful about the human body? Loosen up." One traditional stereotype is "Blacks are simple people; they find pleasure in simple things and don't require many material goods." And a corresponding "in" theme states: "America is wasteful. We have over-produced, polluted, and destroyed. We should live more simply—back to nature: bicycles instead of cars, backpacks instead of suitcases, tents instead of houses." Or finally, and (though many more examples might be given): "Blacks love to sleep, and they'll sleep anywhere at the drop of a hat." And the contemporary chorus resounds: "We gulp too many pills, Nytol, Sleepease, Sominex, Compos, Quiet World, Twilite, and Nervine. If we could find peace we could rest. See your guru for suggestions."

Surely, the stereotyped black man is the vanguard of the future.

If only he exists!

VIGNETTE FIVE

Random House is publishing a series of studies on American ethnic groups, and one of the books in this series is, interestingly enough, on white Southerners. The author is Lewis Killian. Native Georgian and distinguished sociologist, Killian moved from the South several years ago to a position at the University of Massachusetts. There was a reception for new faculty. Several Europeans, with heavy accents, preceded him in the receiving line and were greeted with only the ordinary comments. But when Lewis moved forward and introduced himself, he was asked whether he missed being away from home! This story is told by Peter Rose, who adds: "There are many strangers in the land—including white southerners." The story illustrates an important point that must not escape us: It is not only Southern *blacks* who know the minority experience; the South, in relation to the rest of the nation (parallel to the black man in relation to the white man) has known deprivation, derision, and accusations of immorality and incompetence; and the Southerner (in the folk expression) is "no count." The white Mississippian, too, knows what it is like to shuffle his feet, to be vilified, to be poor and seen as a problem, to come in the back door of the nation and wait around in its kitchen. Here is the foundation for understanding and sympathetic identification among us, though I cannot be confident that the opportunity will be realized.

VIGNETTE SIX

The growing social differentiation in the black community should not pass without notice, since it raises serious questions whether a common racial consciousness and identity can persist. There are those on the make and those in risk of being a permanent underclass, there are increasingly large numbers in secure white-collar occupations with corresponding life styles, and there are those increasingly desperate members who find hope in neither self nor social system. Everything we know about the dynamics of social class suggests that disparate class in-

terests will tend to rupture racial unity, with differences
widening between the views of the black underclass and
those of the black "haves" concerning needed remedies
and proper ventures. Some say that a new, "popular"
leadership is embraced at all class levels, there being an
underlying sense of blackness that overrides the sense of
class. But such a union is fragile, and calling each other
"brother" and "sister" may not be a sufficient glue.

New Perceptions

Certain new perceptions have emerged in the past few
years, issues that were not in our awareness when the
Supreme Court's *Brown* decision was announced in 1954
and which even now have not been clearly defined. Space
does not allow full reflection on these issues, yet I wish
briefly to comment on two: one is the issue of pluralism;
the other is that of competence. They are more interre-
lated than they seem at first glance, and I think I can
discuss them together.

The civil rights movement of the last twenty years
intended to increase freedom and opportunity for blacks
such as would establish parity as between the races. The
attack focused on segregated public institutions where
decisions were made by whites and the system patrolled
by whites. The racial disproportions in privilege and re-
ward were staggering, and they were so obvious that little
time was given to such questions as what goals were
sought and how we would know it when we got to where
we thought we wanted to go.

Some problems emerge now. Let me state one problem in the following abstract manner: Under conditions of equity and justice, in what ways may the races be distinctive, in what ways must they be alike? And a related question: What competencies and skills are essential in all groups if each is to be adequately prepared to compete for the rewards of the society at this time in history?

Let me now take a specific instance. An argument has raged over the meaning and significance of the results of standard academic achievement tests in which the racial gap in performance is very substantial. Whites have tended to take these results at face value and say that they reflect real differences of stunning concern.

Blacks have tended to attack the tests themselves, arguing in effect that the standards of a wholistic society are being imposed on what is in fact a pluralistic situation. Whites may know more about the things the tests test, but blacks know more about many things the tests don't test. According to the argument, there is more need to change the expectations of the judges than to change the behavior of the judged. Indeed, some have gone further to say that black education is a matter for consideration by black decision makers operating community-controlled black schools in which black teachers teach a black curriculum to black students using standards of evaluation determined by the black community. (Those among you who have argued for states' rights against federal usurpation should quickly appreciate this argument.)

Yet let us make a counterargument. Can blacks afford *not* to possess the skills the dominant society rewards? Granted, if the United States were a different kind of society—if it did not emphasize entrepreneurial skills and technology, if it were not metropolitan and industrial, if it did not revere the secular so much and the sacred so little—then different skills would be desired and different kinds of people would be rewarded. As our society exists in fact, however, the verbal and mathematical skills and the substantive knowledge tested on achievement tests have unquestioned importance. If blacks are to secure a fuller share of the rewards that America offers, they must acquire more of the skills that America expects; blacks are not in a position, either from the standpoint of numbers or from the standpoint of power and influence, to have a decisive effect on the nature of those expected skills. Thus the future well-being of blacks in the American class and income structure requires their increasing mastery of the skills and knowledge offered and represented by the schools.

My own expectation is that the pressures toward a single set of standards are inexorable. Those areas of activity and belief known as "black culture" seem likely to me to become increasingly peripheral in the overall picture, as the increasing involvement of blacks in the national economy and educational system reemphasizes standard conceptions of competence. If I am right, then the task of developing the quality of the school performance of blacks compared to whites will be a major national and regional concern in the decades ahead, since the racial gap is now alarming and no solutions are known. But I may be wrong. For example, if we convince ourselves that we are over educated and that educational standards for many jobs are grossly inflated, then other criteria may come to the fore and academic competence recede in emphasis. Whatever the outcome on this particular matter, I suggest to you that the issue of pluralism in our regional society underlies and interprets a number of the concerns that will be upon us in the coming years.

The Problem of Community

Another problem pressing upon us is that of community. We in the South have had a layered system, white on top, black on bottom, yet within the rules and etiquette governing that system we have had a substantial interracial warmth and humanity. These bonds, these common touches of decency, have been bruised and battered as we have grown more urban and more mobile, and as blacks have protested the layered system. But the tradition of warmth, the foundation, is there, as is a grace and a casualness deserving to be prized. This region will remain an *interracial* society; the blacks will not leave, nor will the whites. And it is equally clear that we are not going to be an *assimilationist* society, either North or South; separate ethnic and racial identities will continue in the American stream, whether we talk about Poles and Irish or blacks and whites. The notion of color blindness is as socially unreal as it is perceptually impossible, and it is quite clear that the force of the state is not necessary to maintain racial identity and separate pride. How silly that we should have ever thought so!

I believe that the search for rootedness is a major phenomenon of the modern world. I think it underlies the most disparate phenomena: antique shops and communal movements, genealogical searches and odysseys to Africa, the drug and drink culture and the psychiatrist's couch, photograph albums and the restoration of old houses, the purchase of land and the maintenance of cemeteries. We have learned how silly it is to call America a melting pot in which we all get scrambled up and come out a new amalgamation; in point of fact, Jews remain Jews, and Catholics remain Catholics, and Irish remain Irish. They remain proudly so, sometimes disruptively so, but with net benefit to the flavor of our land. (And we have learned how silly it is to argue that if people sit down in the same classroom they'll get married!) It is a powerful fact of history that when the whites of the South seek the comforts of rootedness and continuity they have nowhere to look save the traditions and heritage of this region.

And poignantly, we say the same of blacks. The black pilgrim to the slave coast of Africa comes back happy that he went but newly convinced that his destiny and his history lie not there but here—in this land, in this soil. Facing our common history, whites must grapple with and respond to the guilt of having bought, sold, separated, abused, and brutalized involuntary residents. Facing that same history, blacks must grapple with and adjust to the uncertain records, the limited material heritage, the inexperience with authority, and the bitter psychic residues that assail the exploited. But it is all we have. And it is not all bad. Blacks persevered and survived under extreme adversity—no mean achievements. Forms of interracial joviality and cordiality true to the prouder human tradition were common, as were tender

alliances and mutual respect. We are not allowed to
handle the past tenderly when revolutionary fervor
reigns. But now in its aftermath there is a time for selec-
tion and choice, for deliberate retrieval from the rubble
even while new structures appear.

And thus I end on an optimistic but somber note.
Terrible things have continued to happen to the world
these past two decades. We have seen even more of man's
organized capacity for inhumanity and bestiality: a sobering experience. And we have seen too, as political conflicts have raged in newly independent nations, that the
victims of historic injustice do not seem reluctant to inflict
injustice themselves when power is theirs. As we have
learned more of the world, we have come to see that the
experiences blacks have endured in slavery and Reconstruction and Jim Crow and Depression and since, though
awful in scope, are not extraordinary in the annals of
anguish. And the modern movements of people, which
bring those of different physical features together in unprecedented numbers and frequency, demonstrate to us
that this Southern region is not unique in strife and bitterness and exploitation when peoples meet.

The just society escapes us all, and seemingly always,
everywhere, there are the victims, the exploited, the
dispossessed—the only uncertainties being, society to
society and time to time, who they will be and the extent
of their misfortune. A steady drumfire against the region's
racial customs has seemed to say that white Southerners
were a peculiarly vile, corrupt, and woebegone people,
and that nothing prideful or redemptive accrued to any
who were its children. We are done with that time for the

most part, let us be thankful. Now we can prepare our balance sheets in more judicious tone. The occasion to see ourselves in perspective is an occasion to rejoice, an opportunity to seize. For as indeed there are in this region's heritage things worth preserving, there is basis for hope that we can create a future satisfying to the human spirit. And as blacks too accept this heritage, recognize that neither Harlem nor Africa is escape, or homeland, and settle in to make do here as best they can, *all* of us may acknowledge that the South is a porous but bounded entity from which we do not escape, and we are free to get on about the business of preserving civility and finding justice.

Comments by WILLIAM C. CAPEL

We now know that America was never a "melting pot," and the idea that there was something in the very presence of our country that would change European peasant immigrants into an amalgamated man, new and superior to the old, was a myth. There has remained a counter theory, that there are cultural variations in our country, and that these variations follow regional lines. We have the shrewd New Englander, epitomized by Senator Aiken, upright and honest, but not above selling a wooden chestnut or two to people from other regions. Then we have the taciturn Westerner, gentle to a fault to women and horses, but fatal to the Indian, the bank robber or the Eastern crook. The South, however, despite its vague geographical boundaries, has had attached to it more myths, legends, and some truths, than other regions, and this particularly applies to states of the Confederacy.

A social phenomenon does not have to be true to be true in its consequences, and whether one believes the Southerner has different genes (superior of course), or has been exposed to a unique life experience, or simply lives in a hot climate, a large percentage of white Southerners believe that they are "different." The "Southern way of life," while it has become a code word for racism, has more meaning than that. This difference, this sectionalism, or, if you will, this orneriness has been subject to much examination; but let us take a brief look at three views, set in different times, and conducted under different circumstances, but all on the same theme.

In the 1920s there was published in Nashville a small literary magazine called *The Fugitive*, whose editor and principal contributors were loosely or intimately connected with Vanderbilt University. It was an exceedingly talented group. John Crowe Ransom, Allen Tate, and Robert Penn Warren composed the core group who drew together a small band of like-minded apostles and wrote *I'll Take My Stand*, a spirited explication of the Southern differentness and a spirited defense of the South, especially of the agrarian tradition and its position vis à vis the Negro. The book created great interest and went through a number of editions and is still used as a good reference about the differentness of the South.

Ten years later, with the great depression intervening, there appeared *The Mind of the South* by W. J. Cash, again pointing out the distinctive qualities of Southern life. This book continues to be used as a standard reference as to the reasons for the South's being different. Recently, in 1972, came John Shelton Reed from Chapel Hill to tell us in *The Enduring South* that our regional subculture, while not wholly intact, has retained much of its peculiar ego and that the mind of the South is alive and well south of the Mason-Dixon Line.

The "Agrarians" of Nashville tried to prove their case by poetic insight and trilling rhetoric; Cash wrote in a polemical, newspaper style, making his case about Southern demagogues and absentee mill owners, while Reed, in the true sociological tradition, invoked the sacred cow of statistical methodology. How then, if we have taken our stand, with a mind which is the South's own and which will endure presumably forever, can we discuss change since 1954 or any other date?

The twelve Agrarians on Nashville's hills in 1930 saw in the South a reflection of the agrarian virtues of the old Roman Republic; Cash saw the South as the oppressed section of a nation, forced by harsh economic necessity to devise a way to survive and endure, while Reed now sees the difference primarily in the institutions of the family and religion having a greater impact in the South and the institutions of education and the media having less impact than in other regions of American society.

In modern societies structural changes have generally been in response to technological changes, which often have unforeseen consequences. It was World War II that made possible the revolution in agriculture, primarily in cotton culture, that so preoccupied Southern thought. Cash devotes only three paragraphs out of some 430 pages to the invention of the first successful cotton picker by the Rust brothers. He noted that the Rust brothers were men of social conscience and proposed that the profits from their invention go to the resettling and rehabilitation of those who would be thrown out of work by its introduction—a noble aim that somehow got lost in the translation by John Deere, International Harvester, and the other final builders of the machine.

If one examines the writings of Vance, Coulter, Woofter, Jóhnson, and Howard Odum, one cannot help noticing the overwhelming concern with the problem of farm tenancy and cotton culture and the subsidiary problems of the cotton mill village. Today these problems, so important to these men, are scarcely mentioned. When we speak of rural poverty it is not tobacco road that comes to mind, but people trying to exist in the backwash of agribusiness and when we speak of the problems of the blacks, we are most usually thinking of the deterioration of the cores of our cities. It was not the *mind* of the South that changed these problems, but technological engineers at their drawing boards.

The many direct results of the *Brown v. Board of Education* decision can be evaluated in terms of successes and failures in educational equality, busing, and racial balance. All of these can become political questions, but none is the significant thing about the *Brown* decision. Its main effect is upon this same differentness that has been so often and well noted. As revisionist historians have shown, Reconstruction in the South was, for the most part, brief and often half-hearted, because basically both sides shared the same beliefs and values about the proper relationships of the races. The generation of school children who have grown up since *Brown* (and remember, even if *Brown* had been fully implemented in 1954, they would only now be juniors and seniors in college) is the first generation to experience the trauma of *failed certainty*. They saw a law imposed on the folkways and mores of their parents (and their teachers as well) and it was not the law that, as in the 1870s, blinked. This generation *knows* that great changes, not only in space flight or in medicine, but in ordinary, day-to-day human relations, can occur and the heavens do not fall, and the earth does not tremble.

Children reared since 1954 have had vastly different conditioning experiences in terms of what constitutes proper roles in life, of how to act the roles of men and women, of what is success, and the like. Assumptions and aspirations no longer are founded in the agrarian tradition, but there has been no true urban substitute. What Riesman called "other-directed," the taking of one's values from one's peers rather than from a fixed tradition, is as strong in Southern youth culture as elsewhere.

What is implied here is that we may be measuring the wrong people, perhaps in the wrong way, and by the wrong standards, if what we are concerned with is change.

For example, Reed's study utilized public opinion polls over the past 30 years, and from this study he draws his conclusions about the strength of family influence; but Reed is not measuring this first post-*Brown* generation, which is also the first suburban Southern generation. For those over forty years of age, there is a wide chasm between the webs of kinship they knew, and those of their children. In one sample of students each one was asked to list all of his relatives who were "blood kin" to him. Eighty percent could name all their grandparents, but less than one-half could name their great-grandparents. Only 40 percent knew the family names of their grandmothers, and a surprisingly large number could not name any of their first cousins. Second cousins might have well been Eskimos and as for a cousin once removed, only 10 percent knew what such a relation was. When we look at student opinions on such questions as sex behavior, drug use, and the like, we find that premarital behavior and drug use in Southern colleges almost exactly match national norms. In short, there is strong reason to believe that there has been a basic change in the assumptions of today's youth that has not yet had time to become fully recognized.

The great significance of the *Brown* decision is that it will become a benchmark, something to which we will more and more relate the withering away of the differences of the South. The Civil Rights Act of 1964 was probably much more immediate in its results, and the vast amount of social legislation subsequent to *Brown* has resulted in greater integration of Southern society, but *Brown* was the event and 1954 was the year that marks the great departure. Whatever the statistical data may show, whether the Coleman report on the apparent failure of compensatory education is correct or not, *Brown* has been a perceived success. One of the most dramatic changes in the history of opinion polling has been the shift of Southern public opinion between 1942 and 1972 on the matter of integration of schools, and whereas over 60 percent of all Southerners objected to blacks and whites attending school together in 1963, only 16 percent do so today.

Add to this the political realignment of much of the South and we can begin to see a picture of greater readiness to accept change since *Brown* demonstrated that social change can occur contrary to the folkways, can be expanded, and can be lived with. A theory in psychology called cognitive dissonance has shown us that if we cannot change a situation we come to accept it and then to love it.

It may well be that much of the old Southern mind was love of a condition from which it could not escape prior to 1954 and that changes since then will occur for the same reason.

In view of what has been said above it would be well to see how this generation of Southerners perceives its heritage before taking a stand on an enduring mind of the South.

V

Sutpen's Door:

The South Since the *Brown* Decision

PAUL M. GASTON

I AM NOT CERTAIN that a historian is the best person to bring either illumination or good cheer out of the history of the recent past. David Donald, for example, pointed out recently that the decline in the reputation of historians over the past generation has caused them to experience a severe "crisis of confidence." Little needed for guidance, they "have lost the general reading public to the amateurs, writers who usually have had no graduate training in history and who hold no university appointments. Books by Bruce Catton and Barbara Tuchman, William Manchester and Walter Lord, are selected by the big book clubs, receive lead reviews in popular periodicals, and win prizes."

Perhaps even worse, "professional historians have also

lost status within the university community. Since the first Russian Sputnik the cushiest professorships, the largest summer-salary supplements have gone to the natural and social scientists. Treated as second-class academic citizens, historians have increasingly come to question the value of their own discipline."

To this lamentable state of affairs some historians themselves have unwittingly contributed. The late Walter Prescott Webb, for example, believed that the historian—and especially the historian of the South—was a positive enemy of progress and therefore a pariah to anyone who wished to hope and plan for a future of happiness and prosperity. Toward the end of his distinguished career, Webb became a propagandist for a new South of progress and prosperity. In the early 1960s I heard him bring his message to Virginia, informing us that "this next century will belong to the South." A man on a mission, he explained that he intended to travel across the region and to tell a story "of cheerfulness, of optimism and hope, a story calculated to lift the spirit, turn the eyes of a Southerner . . . to a future so bright as to be to some all but unbelievable." In such an enterprise, Professor Webb believed that the Southern historian could supply only discouragement because, he explained, the history of the South had been so full of "misfortune, of calamity, of disaster, of catastrophe" that "those who teach [Southern] history and those who study it are likely to be so conditioned by it that they take a somber view of not only the past but also of the future."

Webb's enthusiasm for progress—the persistent temptress of the poor and backward South—seems to me temporarily to have blinded him to the real virtues of his craft. In fact, despite the alarms of Mr. Donald and the admonitions of Mr. Webb, I believe that historians ought to be able to make an important contribution to our understanding of the past two decades in the South and that we ought to make that contribution by remaining loyal to the fundamental creed of the profession—the belief that the materials and the mature interpretation of Southern history are assets, not liabilities, in the struggle to humanize the South and to redirect the priorities of the nation.

The late Richard Hofstadter, whose work touched the South only incidentally, understood this point better than most. Shortly before his death he wrote of the growing frustration in America and of the mounting impatience with anything complicated. "We may expect," he warned, "that the very idea of complexity will itself come under fire once again, and that it will become important for a whole generation to argue that most things in life and in history are not complex but really quite simple." This demand, Hofstadter wrote, "I do not think the study of history can gratify." By its very nature, Hofstadter explained, history—at least history writing as practiced by mature minds—"forces us to be aware not only of complexity but of defeat and failure: it tends to deny that high sense of expectation, that hope of ultimate and glorious triumph, that sustains good combatants." Nor, he added, should this truth be lamented: "In an age when so much of our literature is infused with nihilism and other social disciplines are driven toward narrow positivistic inquiry, history may remain the most humanizing of the arts."

Now, in an interdisciplinary conference such as this I do not wish so baldly to insist upon the primacy of history, but I do believe that, at the least, history ought to provide special ways of coping with the past that can illuminate the problems of the present.

For one thing, Southern historians in particular ought to have a special fondness—a special sympathy—for the ironic interpretation of history implicit in what Hofstadter had to say about the historian's task. Certainly all of the best commentators on the Southern experience have written from that perspective. Most of them—at least most of the best ones—have taken a cue from the writings of William Faulkner. Faulkner's story of the South—and I hope I don't oversimplify too much—is, as Malcolm Cowley pointed out a long time ago, a kind of parable of the fall. Here was a land that offered a fresh start, a life of beauty and integrity and wholeness. But this promise of an idyllic life was spoiled by the ruthless exploitation of both men and land that undergirded the creation of the Old South, and constituted the tragic flaw in all of the region's subsequent history.

This insight, it seems to me, has been built on by all of the best commentators on the region. Among the historians, C. Vann Woodward is the one who has, I believe, developed it most persuasively. And it is also he who has most successfully popularized its most pregnant application—the concept of the burden of Southern history, an historic, collective experience that bears down upon the present of each generation requiring of it that it acknowledge the fact that one cannot escape history, cannot defy the past.

A second dimension of the historian's contribution to understanding of the recent past should derive from his insistence upon the complexity of experience, the tragic dimensions of human history, upon that denial of the "ultimate and glorious triumph" that Hofstadter wrote about. It was this very reality that propagandist Webb repudiated in his pursuit of progress; which denial inevitability must result in obscuring and distorting the human dimension of our history. And surely it is a truism that our lives may be humanized only when we recognize and confront the realities of the past.

Newly Discovered Virtues

The sense of ironic detachment, which I see as the distinguishing characteristic of the best Southern historians, is especially important to us today now that the relationship between the South and the rest of the nation is taking on new, sometimes startling, forms.

Historically, as all of us have long been aware, the South has served in the American mind as a counterpoint to national moods and images. For much of its history, the South in the American imagination has served as a foil to national claims of virtue, innocence, invincibility, and progress.

In the antebellum period the abolitionists were only the most vocal in reminding everyone that only in the South did human slavery exist: the South, therefore, was made to be the counterpoint to the American claim to freedom.

During the Reconstruction era, when America would be remade to be a place of freedom and equal opportunity, it was the South that had to be reconstructed: once again the Southern region was the counterpoint to the American commitment to a free and open society.

In the twentieth century, the South became the "Savage South," the "backward South," the land of "tobacco road," the "Sahara of the Bozart"—all disturbing images that highlighted the larger and more humane American realities (or presumed realities) of abundance, progress, and enlightenment.

During the era of the Civil Rights Movement the region became, in the popular national imagination, the quintessence of evil, and Americans went through an orgy of South-hating. With the evening television news full of graphic accounts of the torture of children and of savage assaults on black people, the South again represented everything reprehensible in the national history and, again, stood as an embarrassment to the American claim of virtue and innocence.

But then a remarkable reversal took place, and in a stunningly short period of time. The South continued to serve as a counterpoint to the national experience but now newly discovered virtues served to highlight newly discovered vices and failures of the nation.

The Watergate scandal, for example, is a good symbolic example of the change that has taken place. Two decades ago I suppose there was nothing more reprehensible than a Southern politician. Blurting out words of defiance, busily framing the Southern manifesto, and resurrecting the ugly doctrine of interposition, they seemed to Americans to be concerned with dreaming up ways of frustrating the national will, getting people back on the plantation, manacled and oppressed. Contrast this image of the Southern politician of the 1950s with the Watergate matinee idols, Ervin, Baker, and Talmadge. None of these people was ever accused of defending the civil rights of black people, but in 1973 they were national heroes: protectors of liberty, seekers of truth, saviors of honesty and integrity; and, in fact, objects of the special admiration of the American left.

The South, in fact, has been asked to play a remarkable new role as model for the nation to emulate. This new version of the old interest in the South as counterpoint was born, I think, not so much out of developments in the South (although they played a part) as out of shifting and drastically altered perceptions of the nation itself. The 1960s, as we can see so clearly now, saw the destruction of the old and comforting myths of American invincibility, opportunity, and virtue—along with the disappearance of a sense of destiny which had distinguished the nation from its beginnings.

Many things contributed to the destruction of these benchmarks. The riots in Watts and Detroit and elsewhere—not to mention the growing Northern hostility to school desegregation—quickly made it apparent that racial bigotry was not a Southern monopoly but a national phenomenon. Even more important, the tragic war in Vietnam gave the lie to the belief, desperately needed by so many people, that this was a nation that, above all others, championed liberty and deserved the plaudits of the rest of the world for its fearless and selfless defense of freedom for all mankind. In addition to this loss of confidence came the increased concern over crime in the streets, urban decay, pollution of the air and water, a loss of a sense of community, and growing mistrust of one individual of another.

Simultaneously, and as a direct consequence of these disturbing trends, Americans began to look differently at the South. In an almost incredibly short period of time the South was pressed into service to provide guides for ways in which racial and urban problems might be resolved and a sense of community restored. It was, as many commentators noted, an altogether novel situation, this growing national attitude that Southerners might be able to teach something useful, might be able, really, to show how men may live harmoniously in a complex, interracial, urban society. Only yesterday Southerners were being told the opposite: that theirs was a barbarous civilization, exhibiting all the qualities of perverseness, backwardness, and cruelty that the nation must avoid.

Go to the Back Door

Now, certainly, all of this should cause historians—all of us, in fact—to have our antennae up. The supreme irony of the present situation should fortify us in our resolve to retain, professionally at least, our sense of ironic detachment.

One certainty that seems to me to emerge clearly from the present situation is that the perennial interest of Americans in the South has not dissipated. Shreve's old question to Quentin is still being asked. For those of you who have read William Faulkner's novel, *Absalom, Absalom!*, you will remember that Shreve, a Canadian boy, a Harvard freshman and a roommate of Quentin Compson of Yoknapatawpha County, Mississippi, in 1910, asked of Quentin, *Tell about the South. What's it like there. What do they do there. Why do they live there. Why do they live at all.*

Quentin's answer to Shreve's question is what *Absalom, Absalom!* is all about and this remarkable novel, although published in 1936, provides the best perspective I know of for talking about the South, even (perhaps especially) the South since 1954.

The answer to Shreve's question is the bizarre story of the House of Sutpen, of the story of innocence destroyed and the struggle to avenge the wound to a young man's pride. Young Thomas Sutpen had come with his family out of the hills of West Virginia in the early years of the nineteenth century and with them had traveled to the Virginia Tidewater country, where his father found employment on a substantial plantation. Taking a message one day to his father, Thomas knocked at the front door of the Big House only to be told by the black servant that he must go to the back door for his kind of errand. This closing of the door in Thomas Sutpen's face is the turning point of the novel just as it may also be taken to be symbolic of the turning point of Southern history.

Young Sutpen could not understand why any man would ask him to go to the back door. In West Virginia, where he came from, there were no back doors and if you could not get in the front door the only place you would enter would be through one of the windows and the only reason you would enter by the window would be if you were stealing something or hiding from somebody and he wasn't stealing anything and he wasn't hiding from anybody; he wanted only to deliver a message to his father.

To avenge the wrong and assuage his wound, Sutpen can think of nothing to do except to become like those who created the world in which shut doors are an essential part. He creates a grand design; a plan to acquire slaves, a great plantation, and family. With these no one would ever shut a door in his face again.

He leaves for Haiti, takes a wife who bears him a son but puts them both aside when he discovers that she is a mulatto. He eventually finds his way to Mississippi where he creates Sutpen's Hundred, brings to it a proper wife who bears him two appropriate children. Eventually his first son, the Negro son, shows up and from Sutpen's failure to recognize his son, grant him only the recognition that he is his father, stems the tragedy of the house of Sutpen.

Once again a door is shut, figuratively this time. We learn from Faulkner of the profound ways in which black and white are linked together and of the perversions that come to their relationship as a consequence of the scheme of life that is built upon exploitation of the land and enslavement of the labor. It is this institutional flaw—the tragic element in all subsequent Southern history—that sours Sutpen's relationship with his issue, prevents him from reaching out as father to son to grant human recognition.

It is in this Faulknerian sense that the *Brown* decision

of 1954 forced the South to confront the burden of its past: to respond in one way or another to the consequences of a history that, in the manner of Thomas Sutpen, embraced the closing of doors on one's own people. In this sense, then, the South was asked in 1954 to open a door, to accept a sense of responsibility for the past, and, by acknowledging the tragic element of its history, somehow to make its society whole.

Southern Resistance to Desegregation

The challenge presented to the South by the *Brown* decision—the opportunity it gave the region to confront its historic burden—was, from a Faulknerian point of view, a flawed opportunity from the outset for the only way in which the region might become whole, might join past and present harmoniously, was to make a moral decision free of outside pressure. I remember, in one of his Charlottesville talks, Mr. Faulkner telling an audience of the rightness of school desegregation and admonishing them that "We got to do this thing; we got to do it because it's right. But we got to do it before the Yankees make us do it." He still had hope; hope that the South might seize upon that bit of voluntary choice that remained to it.

It did not, of course. In the years immediately after the decision the South was to go through shocks and throes and convulsions as every known effort—and some that had never previously been even dreamed of—were used to stifle the promise of the *Brown* decision.

There was violence in abundance. The record of the

first Klan was easily matched and quickly surpassed. Young children were beaten and tormented. Freedom riders, sitters in, demonstrators—all those who placed their bodies on the line for open public accommodations and the elementary rights of citizenship—were tortured and beaten. And then there is the long list of the murdered: William Moore, Medgar Evers, Johnny Robinson, Lemuel Penn, Jimmie Lee Jackson, James Reeb, Viola Liuzzo; and Mickey Schwerner, James Chaney, and Andrew Goodman; the four young girls who were bombed to death in the Birmingham church; and, of course, Dr. Martin Luther King himself in 1968.

To violence was added an unprecedented degree of hatred and suspicion. The previous highwater mark in the antebellum period, reached as a consequence of the response to the abolitionists, was matched and surpassed by the new outburst of sectionalism that made all outsiders suspect. Natives, too—the modern scalawags—were condemned for deviationism, and thousands of families—we don't know how many—suffered rifts, many of which have not yet healed.

Sometimes—frequently, in fact—the fear and mistrust of all the "outsiders," the "enemy," went to absurd lengths. In 1959, for example, the Citizens Council magazine included, under the heading "Here is the Enemy," twenty-seven Protestant, Catholic, and Jewish church and religious organizations. The National Council of Churches was included; the "Methodist Church" was listed as such. Thirteen labor unions were listed. Also included were the National Newspaper Publishers' Association and the Benevolent and Protective Order of

Elks. The Government of the United States was represented in the camp of the "enemy" by the following: Commission on Civil Rights; Department of the Air Force; Department of Health, Education and Welfare; Department of Justice; Department of Labor; Department of the Treasury; General Services Administration; Housing and Home Finance Agency; Interstate Commerce Commission; and the President's Committee on Government Contracts. Interestingly, the enemy status of the Supreme Court and the federal judiciary was apparently taken for granted and did not have to be listed.

The fear of truth and the flight into fantasy were pervasive and disturbing parts of these early years. All unpleasant facts were explained away as aberrations or as part of a subversive anti-American plot. Thus there was the predictable, but absurd, attempt to portray Martin Luther King as a Communist.

Then there was the politics of reaction and waste. The South, as David Potter has so brilliantly shown in his posthumously published *The South and the Concurrent Majority,* has distinguished itself for its ability to exercise Calhoun's concurrent majority; that is to say, to exercise the power of the negative. In this period, the exercise of the negative became a passionate, all-consuming activity with massive resistance as its greatest monument and the determination to close schools rather than desegregate them its test of will.

There was also the cruelty mixed with inhumanity that marked nearly every aspect of the resistance to the confrontation with the South's past. The most poignant pictures I recall are those of the young children, the first in the desegregated schools, receiving the abuse and the torment of the white students and the parents of the white students. Particularly memorable is the picture of the grown women in New Orleans, shouting obscenities at small children who were entering the first desegregated schools there in 1960.

In Advance of the Nation

Now, beside the fury and the passion of Southern resistance the dismantling of the most oppressive features of the racist order must appear unusually striking. In fact, from the historian's point of view (as well as from the point of view of those of us over forty who grew up with the old system), the stunning achievements of the past two decades seem almost incredible. (Needless to say—or almost needless to say—the achievements, when viewed from the vantage point of the oppressed, seem less comprehensive and awesome.)

Consider, to begin with, the fact that we have seen the destruction of the whole fabric of racist law. For three hundred years, more or less, the fundamental law of the South was designed to assure the subordination of black people to white people. That three-century-old heritage has now been discarded, root and branch. In fact, in many respects, the fundamental law of the region, as of the nation, is drawn to prevent such subordination.

Secondly, self-government, the cornerstone on which the Republic was erected, is no longer denied black people. Except for rare intervals in Southern history self-government was not simply out of the reach, but expressly prohibited to blacks. At the beginning of this period, moreover, blacks were, with only minor exceptions, a disfranchised and politically powerless people. By the end of the 1960s—after the efforts of the Voter Education Project, the registration drives, the Selma March, and the Voting Rights Act of 1965—blacks had entered politics on a massive scale so that there are now more than one thousand black elected officials in the region, the black vote has sensitized white politicians, and, in fact, Democratic party politics in the South has become the principal "integrating" institutional force in Southern life today, replacing the civil rights organizations as the forum for racial discussion and action.

The story of public schools—where the revolution began—is a story that, when it is fully told, will illustrate better than anything else, I believe, what really has happened to and in the South. Robert Coles's *Children of Crisis* is a wonderful place to begin. Here one learns about the young children of courage who set out to make a new social order, fearful of the unknown, but liking even less what they did know. Here, too, I think, may be the real beginning of the youth movement, where children began to learn that they had to assume responsibility for their own destiny.

In addition to courage, the story of the schools is also a tale of almost incredible delays and obstacles: ten years after the *Brown* decision, as a matter of fact, there were more black children in segregated Southern schools then there had been in 1954, and only 2¼ percent of the black school population was attending desegregated schools.

Beside the story of delay and resistance the chronicle of

the persistence and dedication of scores of community groups determined to confront, in one way or another, the challenge of desegregation is impressive. Out of a sense of immediacy and necessity communities, all over the region, developed a sense of responsibility, often of considerable pride, as they slowly and gropingly tried to create a new school system. There is much irony in this story, too, because so many Southern communities, by about 1970, had come to the point where they were ready to do more toward achieving an integrated educational system than the federal government was ready to require of them. In fact, just as the Nixon Administration began, out of the exigencies of national politics, to retreat from the national commitment to equal educational opportunity, the South seemed on the verge of making real breakthroughs. As a consequence, many local leaders, far ahead of the administration, suddenly found themselves out on a limb. It was a strange outcome—this discovery that local communities in the South were in advance of the national government in promoting racial equality.

A Limited Achievement

Now, we cannot deny the momentous nature of these and other changes that have swept across the South, changing its very human appearance. Nor can we deny —or even really appreciate, yet—the long-run potential and significance of the development of black leadership during this period. The development of black strength, black pride, all nurtured in the Civil Rights

Movement, was decisive in ᐟaltering the course of Southern history, for it was black leadership (and black followership) not white leadership (or white followership) that broke the logjam of Southern history and forced the nation to view the shame of the past and the racist bedrock of Southern civilization that had been responsible for that shame.

Nor, in saying (as I am going to say in a moment) that not as much has changed as we might think, do I want to underestimate or obscure the emergence and significance of the ethic of an integrated society, of a sense of community, a kind of counter-culture (particularly among young people), that has been one of the primary fruits of the upheaval of the last two decades.

What I would suggest—and this in full awareness of all the changes I have listed—is that the habits as well as the institutions of a complex society cannot be untangled rapidly, even when the process of separation is prosecuted with force, vigor, and imagination. Belatedly, then, we ought to pay our respects to those who have said that stateways can't change folkways. We have seen the proof that stateways can change folkways—no longer can there be any doubt of that. But what we have not paid sufficient attention to is the fact that though they may change them, they may not eradicate all vestiges of them.

The point is made more credible, I believe, if, instead of focusing on the great changes that have taken place in the past two decades, we consider briefly the ways in which so many of the plagues of the past have eluded the schemes and stratagems of all who would reconstruct the South.

Consider health, to begin with. However measured —by disease, malnutrition, as a consequence of poor housing and sanitation, or simply as a product of lack of access to a doctor or medical assistance of any kind—the health of the Southern people is poor, poorer than anywhere else in America. A recent Southern Regional Council report on comprehensive health care, in witness to this unhappy truth, began with the arresting declaration that "In the South today there are ten and a quarter million people living at or below federally defined poverty levels. This represents nearly 20 per cent of the region's population."

Poverty, then, is another grim reminder that much has yet to be changed. With almost one-half of the nation's poor living in the South, this region ("poverty-prone," to use George Esser's term) retains its historic, if undesired distinctiveness. And with the income of Southern blacks only 55 percent that of Southern whites, one can legitimately question the revolutionary consequences so frequently and carelessly ascribed to the civil rights movement.

Not surprisingly, the housing of the Southern people continues to be in inadequate supply: too expensive for the poor, it even yet is often denied black people on the grounds not only of low income, but race as well.

Public schools, twenty years after the *Brown* decision, have not yet—except in some few remarkable instances—recovered from the shock of desegregation. So much time and energy has been wasted in trying to avoid mere physical mixing of students that the job of educating them has scarcely begun. A whole generation of school children, in fact, will pay for the damage their elders did to public education.

Finally, the region is plagued by an economy in which a small number of people own and control a vast share of our resources. Indeed, this second reconstruction of the South, like the first one a century ago, has not only failed to touch the material foundations of Southern society but, in truth, it never had either a program or a will to do so. We have yet to appreciate the ways in which the economic conservatism of the second reconstruction will limit and qualify the alterations I described earlier.

Wisteria or Kudzu?

I'm not entirely clear where this brief recital of conflicting and contradictory developments leaves us—how much it helps us to understand and evaluate what has happened to the region in the past two decades.

I am reminded, in my puzzlement, of Sheldon Hackney's recent observation that there is "a salutary humanistic lesson in discovering the vine of fate entangling Southern history" followed by his confession that "whether that vine is wisteria or kudzu may vary according to ideological taste." My own view is that the vine is woven of both. In any case, the search to discover it forces us to be aware not only of the complexity of human relations and institutional dynamics, but also of the hard facts of defeat and failure alongside dreams of redemption and visions of harmonious community.

I believe that it is only against such a backdrop—that is

to say, only with a view of history informed by ironic detachment—that one can properly appreciate the quality and the importance of the struggle to open the door that was closed in young Thomas Sutpen's face.

It is principled commitment without the knowledge or likelihood of success that is the true mark of honor, and in the history of the South the examples of honor, courage, and compassion—those qualities of human life most universally admired—have appeared most frequently and compellingly in the struggles to open that door.

The history of the past two decades, perhaps more than any other era of Southern history, is potentially ennobling, then, not because of the "progress" that one can measure, but because of the models of commitment and the examples of courage and honor that enriched it, that remain today as sources of pride, to be sure, but also as witness to the fact that a healthy society is one that takes its inspiration not from what has been achieved, but from what remains to be done; from, that is to say, the unfinished and perhaps unfinishable task of accepting the burden of the past.

CONTRIBUTORS

NUMAN V. BARTLEY, Associate Professor of History, University of Georgia; author of *The Rise of Massive Resistance* and *From Thurmond to Wallace.*

RICHARD J. CALHOUN, Alumni Professor of English, Clemson University; coeditor of *The Tricentennial Anthology of South Carolina Literature;* editor of *James Dickey: The Expansive Imagination;* Fulbright-Hays lecturer in Yugoslavia, 1969–70; member, Executive Committee of the Society for the Study of Southern Literature, 1971–74.

ERNEST Q. CAMPBELL, Professor of Sociology and Dean of the Graduate School, Vanderbilt University; President, Southern Sociological Society, 1967–68; author of numerous professional articles and six books, with major emphasis on Southern education and race relations, including *Racial Tension and National Unity.*

WILLIAM C. CAPEL, Associate Professor of Sociology, Clemson University; author of numerous professional articles and collaborator on several sociological works, including *Deviancy and the Family.*

SAMUEL DUBOIS COOK, Professor of Political Science, Duke University; President, Southern Political Science Association, 1972–73; frequent contributor to professional journals and lecturer at some fifty colleges and universities, with emphasis on Negro politics and recent political change in the South; now President of Dillard University.

ROBERT C. EDWARDS, President of Clemson University; member, Southern Regional Education Board (vice chairman, 1969–71); member, Air Force R.O.T.C. Advisory Panel to Secretary of the Air Force (chairman, 1972);

member, Executive Committee of National Association of
State Universities and Land-Grant Colleges.

PAUL GASTON, Professor of History, University of Virginia;
Chairman and Director of Graduate Studies in History,
University of Virginia, 1966–68, 1969–70; author of *The
New South Creed* and numerous professional articles deal-
ing with recent Southern history.

ERNEST M. LANDER, JR., Alumni Professor of History, Clemson
University; author or coeditor of five books, including
*South Carolina: The Palmetto State, Perspectives in South
Carolina History,* and *A Rebel Came Home;* Ful-
bright-Hays lecturer in India, 1966–67, and in Nigeria,
1970–71.

RAY MARSHALL, Professor of Economics and Director, Center
for the Study of Human Resources, University of Texas at
Austin; President, Southern Economic Association,
1973–74; author or coauthor of numerous professional articles and nine books, mainly on labor, including *Labor
in the South, Labor Economics,* and *The Negro and
Apprenticeship.*

ALFRED S. REID, Bennett E. Geer Professor of Literature, Furman University; editor of *The South Carolina Review,*
1968–73; author of three books, including *Yellow Ruff and
The Scarlet Letter.*

JAMES M. STEPP, Alumni Professor of Agricultural Economics,
Clemson University; President of the Southern Regional
Science Association, 1974–75; Vice-President, Southern
Economic Association, 1954–55; coauthor of three books,
including *The Economics of Environmental Quality.*

WALTER SULLIVAN, Professor of Fiction Writing and of Modern
British and American Literature, Vanderbilt University;
author of two novels, *Sojourn of a Stranger* and *A Long,
Long Love,* and a volume of literary criticism, *Death by
Melancholy.*

INDEX

Afro-American literature, 69
"Agrarians," the, 57, 89, 90
Aiken, George, 88
American Historical Review, 6–7
Anderson (S.C.), planning study of, 48;
    black employment in, 48–49
Askew, Reuben, 25

Baker, Howard, Jr., x, 101
Bartley, Numan V., vii, viii, 20;
    biographical sketch of, 115
Bishop, Paula, xi–xii
Black community, social differentiation
    in, 80–81
Black employment, opportunities of, ix;
    limited improvement in, 28; integration
    in textiles of, 29; patterns around 1950
    of, 30–35; racial discrimination in,
    32–33; effects of migration on, 34–35;
    changes since 1950 of, 35–43;
    agricultural changes of, 35–37;
    discrimination in industry of, 37–38;
    public policy toward, 38–39, 40–42;
    metropolitan patterns of, 39–40;
    opportunities in government jobs of,
    40–41; influence of education on,
    42–43, 45; union influence on, 43;
    conclusions about, 43–46; patterns in
    Anderson (S.C.) and Sumter (S.C.) of,
    48; increasing opportunities in South
    Carolina of, 52–54
Black Employment in the South, 35
Black separatism, 77
Blacks, in novels of 1920s, 1930s, and
    early 1940s, 59–60; in recent fiction, 63,
    64; white stereotypes of, 78–79
Bourbon Democrats, 21
Brooks, Cleanth, 57
Brown v. Board of Education, Topeka,
    vii, viii, x, 1, 3, 10, 13, 27, 33, 56, 59,
    81, 91, 93, 95, 104, 105, 109, 110, 112
Burdette, Mac, xii
Burkette, Sandra, xii

Caldwell, Erskine, 57
Calhoun, John C , 69
Calhoun, Richard J., xii; biographical
    sketch of, 115

Campbell, Ernest Q., vii, ix, 73;
    biographical sketch of, 115
Camus, Albert, 18
Capel, William C., vii, ix–x, 88;
    biographical sketch of, 115
Cash, W. J., x, *The Mind of the South*, 89
Catton, Bruce, 95
"The Central Theme of Southern
    History," 7
Charleston (S.C.) voters, party affiliation
    of, 24
Citizens Councils' enemies list, 106–7
Civil Rights Act of 1964, ix, 28–29, 44;
    effect on Southern literature, 56
Civil Rights Movement, 10; recent
    problems in, 81–84, 100, 110–11
Clemson University, symposium of the
    College of Liberal Arts of, vii, 1; Alumni
    Loyalty Fund of, xii; racial
    desegregation of, 1; changes in past 20
    years of, 2–3
Coleman report, 93
Coles, Robert, *Children of Crisis*, 109
Columbia (S.C.) voters, party affiliation
    of, 23, 24
Compromise of 1877, 9
Compson, Quentin, 103–5
Concept of burden of Southern history, 98
Conrad, Joseph, 63, *Under Western
    Eyes*, 65
Constitutional Convention of 1787, 8
Cook, Samuel DuBois, vii, viii, 5, 21, 26;
    biographical sketch of, 115
Coulter, E. Merton, 91
Cowley, Malcolm, 60
Cox, H. Morris, xi

Dabbs, James McBride, *The Southern
    Heritage*, 76
Davidson, Donald, 57, 59
Dickey, James, 66, 70, 71
Dixiecrat movement of 1948, 9
Donald, David, 95, 97
Doyle, Bertram W., *The Etiquette of Race
    Relations in the South*, 74
Dunn, Charles W., xi
Durham, W. Harry, xi

117